Havoc in the Hub

Havoc in the Hub

A Reading of George V. Higgins

PETER WOLFE

LEXINGTON BOOKS

A division of
ROWMAN & LITTLEFIELD PUBLISHERS, INC.
Lanham • Boulder • New York • Toronto • Plymouth, UK

LEXINGTON BOOKS

A division of Rowman & Littlefield Publishers, Inc.
A wholly owned subsidiary of The Rowman & Littlefield Publishing Group, Inc.
4501 Forbes Boulevard, Suite 200
Lanham, MD 20706

Estover Road
Plymouth PL6 7PY
United Kingdom

British Library Cataloguing in Publication Information Available

Library of Congress Cataloging-in-Publication Data

Wolfe, Peter, 1933–
  Havoc in the hub : a reading of George V. Higgins / Peter Wolfe.
    p. cm.
  Includes bibliographical references and index.
  ISBN-13: 978-0-7391-2150-4 (alk. paper)
  ISBN-13: 978-0-7391-2151-1 (alk. paper)
  ISBN-10: 0-7391-2150-2 (pbk. : alk. paper)
  ISBN-10: 0-7391-2151-0 (pbk. : alk. paper)
  1. Higgins, George V., 1939—Criticism and interpretation. I. Title.
  PS3558.I356Z95 2007
  813'.54—dc22

                                                         2007032763

Printed in the United States of America

♾™ The paper used in this publication meets the minimum requirements of American
National Standard for Information Sciences—Permanence of Paper for Printed Library
Materials, ANSI/NISO Z39.48–1992.

To the loving memory of my brother, Wally

Walter E. Wolfe (1938–80)

Master of Tath and virtuoso of the root, the pit, and the dirt

Contents

Abbreviations

Throughout the text, parenthetical references to Higgins's work will use the following abbreviations.

A	*The Agent*
END	*At End of Day*
BL	*Bomber's Law*
CG	*A Change of Gravity*
CE	*A Choice of Enemies*
CH	*A City on a Hill*
CT	*Cogan's Trade*
DBR	*Defending Billy Ryan*
DG	*The Digger's Game*
D	*Dreamland*
Easiest	*The Easiest Thing in the World*
FEC	*The Friends of Eddie Coyle*

FRN	*The Friends of Richard Nixon*
I	*Impostors*
JDH	*The Judgment of Deke Hunter*
KD	*Kennedy for the Defense*
MT	*The Mandeville Talent*
OW	*On Writing*
O	*Outlaws*
PG	*The Patriot Game*
PJK	*Penance for Jerry Kennedy*
PS	*The Progress of the Seasons*
RF	*The Rat on Fire*
SNFD	*Sandra Nichols Found Dead*
SF	*The Sins of the Fathers*
SS	*Style Versus Substance*
SWAN	*Swan Boats at Four*
T	*Trust*
V	*Victories*
WY	*Wonderful Years, Wonderful Years*

Acknowledgments

The author and publisher join hands in thanking those whose time and energy went into the preparation of this book: Patrick Scott, director of the rare book collection at the University of South Carolina's Thomas Cooper Library, and his fine aide Jeffrey Makala, both of whom helped me access the George V. Higgins file at the Cooper Library; the University of Missouri-St. Louis's first-rate librarians Tim Nelson, Lindsay Schmitz, and Mary Zettwoch; Higgins's patient, cooperative widow, Loretta; UMSL's Mark Burkholder, Barbara Kachur, and John Mulderig, for their help in funding my Higgins project; Jane L. Williamson, whose literary insights improved the project at every stage; Retta Cardwell, for her invaluable help preparing the typescript for publication; and Erwin H. Ford II, Higgins's biographer and top authority on the canon, for leading me to important discoveries. The combined help of the following amounts to a major contribution: Tom Roedel, Sid Edwards, Tory Kaufmann, Eddie De Kalb, Roland McClelland, Julian Fleischman, Carol Warner, Pete Watson, Wade Bingham, and Joe De Rita.

Chapter One

A Nose for Danger

Both comfortable and confident in our world of deeds, George Vincent Higgins rarely felt the need to mince, hedge, or put up his guard. This same cool poise also gave him the flexibility to shift contexts and mind-sets. After earning an MA in creative writing at Stanford and then a law degree at Boston College, he both defended *and* prosecuted litigants at the state and federal levels. No fluke here; he excelled at trial law from the start. During his time in Washington, D.C., he defended Watergate burglar Gordon Liddy and Black Panther Eldridge Cleaver. What a rich, varied career he had. He was a journalist in Providence, Boston, and Washington, D.C. While writing a book a year, he also taught law at both Northeastern University and Boston College. The city of Boston claimed him at the end. After giving up the private law practice he had started in 1983, this long-term resident of Milton, Massachusetts, taught creative writing at Boston University. The many forms his own writing took earned him his professorship. Not only did he write twenty-five novels; his corpus also includes two books on politics, a 1975 study of Watergate, a 1984 takedown of ex-Boston mayor Kevin White, a meditation on his beloved Boston Red Sox, and a sharp treatise on writing. Through it all, his short work appeared regularly in high-profile magazines like *Playboy* and the *Wall Street Journal*, along with the *Boston Phoenix*, a weekly free paper.

Perhaps most remarkably, he enjoyed the buzz, getting as much fun out of writing as he did from lawyering.[1] The elegant meals he took at Boston's Locke Ober Café, together with the boats and sports cars he owned, describe him as extroverted and outward bound. The description holds. The intuitive sense of his roots that flavor his books skirts the Puritan self-criticism that dogged his fellow New Englanders Hawthorne and Henry James. An inheritor of Whitman's optimism, he shrugged off constraints and regrets. Fourteen unpublished novels preceded the appearance of the gangster-driven *Friends of Eddie Coyle* (1972), his first and still best-known full-length work. *Dreamland* (1977), which he disclaims as "difficult and inaccessible" but which H. M. Ruppersburg hails as "a major achievement,"[2] comes to us from the standpoint of a member of Boston's social elite. Writer's block never stopped this prose master whose daily output of pages came to ten, twenty, or even, when he was hot-wired, a hundred.

1

What's more, he controlled this mighty flow. Ward Just's review of the posthumously published *Easiest Thing in the World* (2004) notes the tremendous learning that imbues his fiction. Sound craftsmanship, we may add, kept this learning from becoming intrusive. Higgins wouldn't let it. His advice, proffered several times in *On Writing* (1990), that any writer must read his prose aloud before submitting it for publication, reflects a poet's awareness of the rhythms and tactile values of words.[3] The blend of mood, tone, and character in his prose stems from hard work. Let nobody dismiss George V. Higgins as a wild, untutored prodigy whose inner radar found the mark all the time.

What he *can* be called defies categories. Though he changed the face of American crime fiction, he resented being called a crime novelist (Williams 205). His resentment confirms the happy truth that genius thwarts pigeonholing; Higgins's noncompliance bespeaks originality, too; he writes books that follow their own rules, and that's that. Some of his enigma fades, though, when he's placed alongside an earlier writer who, like him, gloried in the rough-and-tumble of Boston politics in the post-Yankee Protestant age. A scene in *A Choice of Enemies* (1984) takes place in a bar called The Last Hurrah in Boston's Parker House. Higgins also mentions Edwin O'Connor's most famous novel in *Style Versus Substance, Defending Billy Ryan,* and *Swan Boats at Four.*[4] And the motif of the wayward son from O'Connor's 1956 bestseller reappears in Higgins's *Dreamland, Penance for Jerry Kennedy, Wonderful Years, Wonderful Years,* and *Victories.*

Higgins learned from O'Connor. Besides sharing an interest in local politics, the two men, cradle Catholics both, loved baseball, wrote for newspapers and magazines, sometimes about television, and, in their fiction, withheld judgment from their sometimes nasty characters. Other comparisons come forth. The father-son clash in O'Connor's *I Was Dancing* (1964) recurs in Higgins's Jerry Kennedy novels and *Victories* (1990). But unlike Higgins, O'Connor inclined toward nostalgia and sentimentality, a trait seen in his penchant for writing about old men who could also be widowers, like the exuberant Frank Skeffington of *The Last Hurrah.* If these lovable elders are few in number, their scarcity reflects the truth that the slow-working O'Connor wrote far fewer books than Higgins. But the time he spent away from his desk served him well. His courtly upper-class bearing won him dinner invitations to both the White House and the Vatican. These honors lost their gleam, though, along with the lesser ones enjoyed by his more prolific counterpart. Oddly, both men died relatively young, soon before a decade birthday. The nonsmoking teetotaler O'Connor (1918–68) never made fifty, whereas Higgins (1939-99), who gave up cigarettes but kept drinking, died a few weeks short of sixty.

Still worse, the books of these gifted writers are largely forgotten today. There's reason to think that this injustice will be redeemed. An intuitive grasp of their roots helped both men write with aplomb about what they knew. But the comparison ends here. Higgins writes with more grace and verve than

O'Connor. The more natural writer, he crafts work that's clear, unhurried, and seemingly effortless. Such is his genius that he also delivers more than fast, entertaining stories. He writes like a poet, both at the level of the sentence and that of overall narrative pattern; without looking deliberate and pored over, his books reveal careful planning. They also include recurrences, countering motifs, and parallels, which mesh all the more smoothly for being allowed to breath without any nagging authorial insistence upon meaning. Most of the time, Higgins's fiction shows inspiration and originality trumping sophistication; the pull of storytelling gives his work freshness and bounce. He's a quick study in novelistic self-trust. No need for him to pose or show off when he can call up the densely layered insights lodged in both his conscious and unconscious. Writing is what he did and who he was.

I

He was born in Brockton, Massachusetts, and grew up in nearby Rockland. This background makes his knowledge of Boston, the setting for most of his work, fresh and first hand, which, in turn, helps explain the gusto, verve, and accuracy that infuse his descriptions of the town. Rather than explaining Boston to outsiders, he has put himself in its offices, stores, and cafés alongside his townsfolk, happy to be on a level with them.

Would that this joy traveled well. The vividness of his Boston-set work clashes with the pallor and staleness clouding his treatment of Washington, D.C. in the two early novels, *A City on the Hill* (1975) and *A Year or So with Edgar* (1979). Why this artistic comedown? In 1974, he published *Cogan's Trade*, the third installment of a triumphant breakthrough series of short novels built around lowlife Boston hoods. One glowing review of the books followed another, in the UK as well as the United States; Higgins gave well-received interviews both in print and on TV; his short work broke into *Esquire* and *Atlantic*. But this acclaim put him at a crossroad. Though he enjoyed celebrity, he also saw the dangers of paying for it with formula writing. Yes, the formula was working well. But it also distracted and later deterred this ex-English major son of two English teachers.[5]

No writer ever grew by working from the cozy middle of his talent. The challenge of the new always charmed the adventurous Higgins. But he erred by attempting mainstream fiction while also moving his narrative base to D.C., where he had spent less time and which he knew less well than Boston, the seedbed of his art. As a result, his presentation of D.C. is willed rather than instinctual. *City* and *Edgar*, written while Higgins was working on Watergate, scrape the bottom of his canon, the zesty, robust speech of their predecessors trailing off to "a know-it-all manner foisted on characters of higher social status."[6]

The social elite also people Higgins's Boston-set work, but their Beacon Street aura mingles with the fumes beating out from Boston's mobbed-up North End and the tough Irish "Southie" district. John Williams may have had this multicultural brew in mind when he referred to the "half-assed, half-European city of Boston."[7] Social distinctions may be sharper in the Hub than in any other major American city (think the High Church Cabots, Lodges, and Back Bay; think Rocky Marciano, Marvellous Marvin Hagler, and Boston's rapscallion four-term mayor, James Michael Curley).[8] Higgins maps Boston society, sometimes in the same novel. His Jerry Kennedy's heart may lie with the thugs he defends in court. But, like Ross Macdonald's Lew Archer, he can also talk to people from all social levels, and he can go anywhere at least once. This social mobility furthers in Higgins the development of that Dickensian motif brought into American popular fiction by the Californians Dashiell Hammett, Raymond Chandler, and Ross Macdonald—the spreading stain; a small, routine-looking disturbance will portend an acute disorder swathing miles and plaguing generations of families.

Elmore Leonard's tag for Higgins, "the Balzac of Boston," pegs into this trauma.[9] A commonplace routine, like sorting the day's mail, which for most of us consists of throwaways, warrants Higgins's attention in *Swan Boats* because it supports a reality we share and identify with. This commonality also fits Boston, a city whose smallness and interconnectedness serve Higgins better than the larger, more sprawling and tentacled New York: "Greater Boston [said Higgins in 1988] is a . . . collection of once-distinct villages. Panic becomes epidemic in such settings, which is why witches were stoned and hanged in seventeenth-century Salem."[10] Higgins has grazed former House Speaker Thomas P. "Tip" O'Neill, Jr.'s belief that all politics are local. His flair for local details, his vivid theatricality, and his ability to probe the personalities of his people all convey both the buzz and the dark backstory of his hometown. What's more, he delivers this complex, closely knit reality without making it look merely picturesque or local-colorful. Credit his tact, too; no secular preacher, he. He'll neither patronize the lunch-bucket constituency that kept re-electing Tip O'Neill and James Michael Curley nor shake an angry fist in the direction of the genteel old Anglo-Brahmins John P. Marquand scathed in *The Late George Apley* (1937).[11]

Mood and atmosphere outpace plot and anecdote in Higgins. The speaking voice in his best work both springs from and defines working-class Boston, a landscape of sad streets, shingle homes, and battered cars. Higgins sets down in this grim subculture, describes it, and, often, leaves it nastier than it was before. Some of its inhabitants or alums are priests (*The Digger's Game, The Patriot Game, The Mandeville Talent*); some work in media (*A Choice of Enemies, Impostors*); some enforce the law (*The Judgment of Deke Hunter, Bomber's Law, At End of Day*). Nearly all would be familiar to moviegoers who saw *Good Will Hunting* (1997), *Mystic River* (2003), and *The Departed* (2006). Higgins's Boston is a cramped, exhausting and overpowering city that wrecks dreams. Its stressfulness comes largely from the problems posed by its ubiquitous traffic jams. It takes so long to drive into metropolitan Boston that, once there, cranky motorists stay put rather than risk narrow, grid-blocked streets to visit other parts of town. Nor has suburban expansion eased the stress, characters in *Eddie Coyle*, *Outlaws*, and *The Agent* spending long numbing hours behind the wheel. (On the dedication page of *The Progress of the Seasons* [1988], Higgins calls the family car one of the three places where his mother "spent most of her life.")

Crystallizing Higgins's love-hate bond with Boston is his steamy response to the Red Sox. The "ill-starred but beloved" Sox can "cloud . . . minds" (SS 29,12) all over New England, he said in 1984. The many snide, angry references to the team in the canon show them vexing Higgins, as well. The Sox riled not only him, though, but also his father and grandfather, with whom he saw his first game at Fenway Park, an outing that might not have been a total joy. "My grandfather used to bang the chair arm and shout when the Sox were playing badly,"[12] Higgins recalls. Grandpa Charlie's woes reverberated. *Progress* depicts the team as more of a local obsession than a diversion, Charlie's grandson bemoaning mishaps on the field, blunders made by the front office, and the farm system's failure to develop talent. He even speaks of deserting the Sox after the 1986 season because the team, wasting a golden chance to win the World Series, "exceeded the limit of his ability to endure pain" (PS 183). A judge's reference in *Outlaws* (1987) to "those blasted Red Sox" (65) strikes a chord with the jurors he's addressing. Their allegiance to the infuriating Sox has prepared them for the loss of both wages and time with loved ones imposed by jury duty; any Red Sox fan knows the feeling of haplessness.

The writing of *Progress* didn't quiet Higgins's fury, which, first stoked at age six, heated up during the eight or ten annual visits he made to Fenway as an adult. The rage even burns into the deep structure of his novels. In a brilliant stroke of foreshadowing, a homicidal gas station attendant enters *A Choice of Enemies* (in chapter 11) while watching a Sox game on a TV screen that's as cloudy and broken up as his mind. But the tormented Roger Knox comes to us only as a Sox fan, perhaps even a representative one, until he's named (his last name incidentally rhyming with Sox) in chapter 19 (87, 205).

That Roger makes his lone visit to metropolitan Boston to murder his brother-in-law evokes the truth that Higgins's home team rarely consoles or comforts. But malice can cause trouble anywhere in the Hub, as is shown in the following scene from *Trust* (1989), which unfolds miles away, at New York's JFK Airport. The portent the scene exudes gains menace from Higgins's treatment, which feeds our taste for exoticism without flattening his Bostonians into exhibits in a freak show:

> Earl found a space . . . in the domestic airlines terminal building. . . . He uncovered a . . . camera with a 135-mm telephoto lens attached, a 28-mm wide-angle lens, and a 50-mm normal lens. There were three unopened boxes of Kodak Tri-X 24-exposure film. He opened one of them and took out the

canister. He took the film cartridge out of the canister and loaded it into the
camera. . . .
He found a place to stand on the second floor—Departures. . . . He . . . made
sure of his sight lines and surroundings. [13]

We've been snared. The passage, with its attentiveness to technical details, has
both said more than we need to know and withheld vital information. We're not
told, for instance, why the pictures that Earl Beale is preparing to snap
warranted his long drive to JFK from Boston. Yet Higgins's parallel phrasing
conveys a control and consistency on Earl's part that lend the photo-op dramatic
weight. The subject-verb-object movement of most of the sentences, all of
which start with the pronoun, "He," shows Earl giving every aspect of his job
equal weight, as if scamping the tiniest detail might sink the job. Earl knows
what he's doing. And so does Higgins, making us read another four pages and
thus deepening our commitment to the book, before divulging Earl's motives.

Which, being venal and treacherous, square with the many images of urban
decay set forth in Higgins's work; patchy renewal in the form of houses with
sagging front porches and jerry-built welfare apartment buildings seen in slate-
gray, rain-drenched light thwart cheer. Nor apparently does the noonday sun
brighten matters. Under a glaring sky full of pigeons, which a character calls
"flying rats" (FEC 38), Higgins evokes the spookiness of midday in a busy
downtown neighborhood where everyone besides the panhandlers and "Jesus
screamers" (FEC 34) is working, shopping, or having lunch.

This scene in the Common evokes the spiritual dementia of the age without
smuggling in myth or ideology. Higgins's art of avoidance rests on his belief,
stated in *On Writing*, "True art is knowing when to stop" (173). He needs no
safety net in the form of magic, fantasy, or holy writ. In his hands, less can do
the work of more. The sense of identity loss and the figure of the protagonist-in-
exile set forth by bleak, maze-like Boston fuse with an urban literary continuum
that swathes Dostoevsky and Don De Lillo as well as James Joyce; Eddie
Coyle's canvassing of Boston to find ways to avoid prison makes him a high-
anxiety version of Joyce's Leopold Bloom in *Ulysses*.

By sending him through Boston's streets and dives, Higgins isn't writing
counterfactual history. Any number of characters in novels like *Dreamland*,
Outlaws, and *Sandra Nichols Found Dead* (1996) who project old-money and
prep-school clout perform deeds as wicked as those done by the brilliantly
named Michael "Mikey-Mike" Magro of *The Digger's Game* (1973) and *The
Patriot Game* (1982), Salvatore "Seats" Loblanco of *Game*, and John "Jack
Bonnie" Bonaventre of *Defending Billy Ryan* (1992). Besides imparting
documentary flair, such names reflect Higgins's close, accurate take on Boston's
underclass. His instinct for the nuances and subtle shifts in social interaction
also shows crime razing social divides. Again, his graceful, economic style bears
thematic weight. Crime in his work unfolds so matter-of-factly that it knits with

money and old family. The two realms coexist seamlessly. Markie Trattman of *Cogan's Trade* (1974) runs a card game from a cheap motel near Bedford, Massachusetts, off of Route 128. The middle-class cops Deke Hunter of *The Judgment of Deke Hunter* (1976) and Harry Dell'Appa of *Bomber's Law* (1993) both married into good families whose scions would shriek were they to learn of their upstart-in-laws' easy ways with crooks. In *At End of Day* (2000), big-time racketeers are so snug with the FBI chiefs pledged to stop them that they've been holding ritual dinners with them for a decade.

Skullduggery in Higgins's Boston takes many forms and exists in so many different combinations that its presentation is never repetitive or one-track. When it bares the strong tie between the Catholic Church and politics, it soothes and disturbs at the same time. The folly of taking the Chinese-American teenager Kitty Lee to Miami eight years before the present-tense action of *The Digger's Game* would have both sent Jerry "Digger" Doherty to jail and cost him his marriage. But his priest-brother Paul not only used his influence with Boston's clergy to help Jerry; he also paid Jerry's legal fees. A big-time hood in *The Patriot Game* wears his tasseled Gucci loafers (always a mark of elegance in Higgins) with confidence. And why not? Both the photos of him taken next to Richard Cardinal Cushing and the trophies from powerful Catholic groups adorning his office spell out his immunity from the law.[14]

Higgins makes us breathe the air of Boston's underworld, an insidious milieu that collapses moral distinctions and, because of his James Ellroy-like weakness for the rank-in-filers of organized crime, lends standing to otherwise obscure places and people. He has twisted the American myth of boundless possibilities and freedom into a microcosm of small-time crime. Defending G. Gordon Liddy during the Watergate trials showed Higgins how this microcosm tallies with the avarice informing public policy at the national level. In a 1986 interview held in Denver, he called avarice a defining human trait: "I believe that while we all like to give an appearance of virtue and morality," he said, "most of us have a price. We would sell out if we got what we wanted."[15]

This cynicism hasn't soured him; he engages with people without expecting much from them. Rather than retreating from ugliness, he immerses himself in it without becoming its devil's advocate. His knack of crystallizing our vague suspicions about human depravity, in fact, discloses in him the self-detachment of a mystic. Both piercingly strange and naggingly familiar, his Boston is a place you've never been, yet would swear you'd seen before. This is a world you can smell and taste as well as feel. Part of the genuineness is ethnic. If wrongdoing can infect national politics, as it does in *The Friends of Richard Nixon* (1975) and *Dreamland* (1977), it can easily corrupt Boston's Italian North End and Irish Southie. Suggesting this fusion is the gangster Donnie Doyle of *Deke Hunter*, who was born Dominic Tesso.[16] *Wonderful Years* (1988) includes two collaborating felons called Sonny Donovan and Frank Leonetti.

Higgins's imagination hasn't played him false. The big-time crooks in his final novel, *At End of Day*, Arthur McKeon (or McKeach) and Nick Cistaro, have as their real-life counterparts James "Whitey" Bulger and Stephen Flemmi.

The shamrock joins with the olive vine on both sides of the law. Two cops named Mickey Sweeney and Donald Carbone team up in *Deke Hunter*, as do Harry Dell'Appa and Bob Brennan in *Bomber's Law*. In fact, crime, its pursuit, and its adjudication have grown so trans-ethnic that *Impostors* (1986) includes a Bedford law firm called Geoghagen and Ramos. This multiculturalism carries forward. Because Quebec stands closer to Boston than Latin America, the French influence in Higgins's fiction outstrips the Hispanic. *Impostors* slots in characters named Timmy Lavalle and Didi Cheneviot. Men named Maurice, Jean, and Henri enter the action on the book's same page (40). The agent in *The Agent*, Alexander Drouhin, has as his chief of staff one Peter Martigneau, and a policeman named Gagnon will investigate his murder. In chapter 2 of Higgins's 1999 novel, a hockey player called Jean Methodiste says of the team he wants to sign with, "They have need of me," inflecting directly from the French (*"ils ont besoin de moi"*) instead of speaking conversational English. On the next page, Jean does speak French.[17]

Unlike him, many of the native speakers of English in the canon talk in a fluid demotic idiom that Higgins has transformed and elevated into an art. Matthew J. Bruccoli's reference to "Higgins's extraordinary skill with American speech and dialogue"[18] stands as one of many tributes to his man's genius with Boston crimespeak. But Bruccoli and Higgins's other partisans would agree that speech is only one of the cultural products, along with Boston's streets, traditions, and institutions (like the Red Sox and parochial education), that Higgins has revamped for our consumption. The preponderance of talk in his work shrinks the distance between him and his people; his allowing the people to speak for themselves puts him on their level. They're not portrayed as quaint eccentrics or dangerous primitives we might either cringe from or laugh at. The banalities of Higgins's criminal class depict lives spinning out of control.

These lives could graze or even collide with our softer, more secure, ones. As the first sentence of *Eddie Coyle* warns, this contact might also put us at risk: "Jackie Brown at twenty-six, with no expression on his face, said that he could get some guns" (3). Like his fellow thugs, Jackie is amoral, the flat, casual tone ("some") of his utterance voicing the detachment of the technician or child who flouts standards of conduct. But he's also feigning the nonchalance of the businessman who's doing his would-be client a favor by trading with him. We know that we should give both him and his arsenal wide berth. We're already feeling the pressure exerted by the motif of the spreading stain. The broader geographical range of Higgins's later work creates patterns that frame Jackie's amorality in a more alarming national context. Jackie's gun-dealing may stand closer than we suspect to the boondoggling hatched in the Vermont statehouse of *Trust* (1989) and *Victories* (1990) and in the D.C.-based *City on a Hill* and *A Year or so with Edgar*. The stain darkens as it spreads. Advisedly, Higgins sets most of the action of *Swan Boats* (1995) on an Atlantic liner en route to New York Harbor and, four years later, that of *The Agent* around a sports agent whose job takes him all over the country. He's putting his readers on notice: we have nowhere to hide. And the reference point of his warning is the Irish-Catholic working-class Boston of his first three novels. This "continuing epic of New England low life and public life," to quote John Williams,[19] will hold solid as long as William F. Kennedy's Albany and John Gregory Dunne's Los Angeles.

II

Storytelling that's done right isn't escapist. By externalizing our inner lives, it brings us as close as we can get to reality. Thanks to his nose for danger, Higgins engages us. The law, as this member of the Massachusetts Bar, practicing attorney, and law professor knows, can quiet our fears of being trampled by forces we may have set in motion ourselves. But we sometimes forfeit legal redress. A misstep by Eddie Coyle that sent another gangster to jail brought harsh punishment down on him. He had his fingers crushed in a door, an act, Eddie assures us, that "[h]urt like a fucking bastard" (FEC 4). Eddie never protested his punishment. The second chapter of End of Day shows enforcer Nick Cistaro visiting a chic Newberry Street art dealer who has reneged on a loan. Backgrounded by the music of Bach, the dealer's elaborate, extended explanation of why his large-scale international business often leaves him short of ready cash fails to move the loan-sharking Cistaro. He doesn't care if Crawford's money is tied up. Crawford has defaulted on a loan, which he must repay, outlandish interest rate and all.

Cistaro's mauling and choking of Crawford, while, advisedly, addressing him "as though disciplining a generally good dog that had oddly misbehaved,"[20] shows the hapless dealer that his debt to the mob calls for prompt action. Crawford slouches back to his studio several hours later with the money he was told to produce. He has learned his lesson: anyone who wrongs or defies the mob will regret it. The lesson holds. Cistaro's partner McKeach has no moral objection to a hoodlum's using a warehouse under his watch as a staging point to distribute drugs. Junius Walter dies because he laughed off McKeach's demand for both rental and protection money.

Such Realpolitik gives Higgins's work the look of a reverse comedy of manners. Vanity and affectation do come to the fore in End of Day and Eddie Coyle, but only to get an unexpected twist. These character flaws, rather than facing ridicule, emerge as essentials in a gangster's code of survival. A mobster's image is his reality. To stay in business, he has to back his tough talk with the threat of swift, remorseless retribution. The ability to punish offenders counts as good business; mob clients or functionaries who know that crossing the mob could kill them dead usually snap into line quickly. A desperate simplicity informs mob justice, as a Mafia capo makes clear in Penance for Jerry Kennedy: "Nunzio is fair," says one of his junior officers. "If he tells you something, and you do not listen to him, a bad thing will happen to you."[21]

As Crawford, the loan-defaulting art dealer in *End of Day*, learns, even though Nick Cistaro can't sue him for nonpayment, he can clarify the advantages of squaring accounts. Cistaro manhandled Crawford just enough to show him that paying his debt beats losing an ear or being dropped into the Charles River shod in cement. Cistaro wasted little effort on Newberry Street making Crawford understand that he was transacting business rather than airing a grudge. To uphold their no-nonsense image, enforcers like Cistaro never let a defaulter slide, even if he's hiding an ocean away. To do so could hurt business.

But doing business Mafia-style violates the law. The strong-arm tactics of organized crime have no place in civilized society. The need to block them calls for a justice system that's precise and responsible. Tradition has always demanded it. Ideally, the law moves from confusion to clarity, coherence, and fairness. The attainment of this goal, the attorney Higgins knows, hinges on the investigation of motive, probability, and sequence. But he also knows that that the shakiness of these guidelines of crime-stopping can hobble the pursuit of justice.

Good law enforcement depends upon the efficiency of the police, an underappreciated, overworked lot whose woes and hardships Higgins sympathizes with, as the following passage from *The Friends of Richard Nixon* (1975) makes clear:

> [C]ops . . . have to see the corpses; console the next of kin; assist to the hospital those who have been raped, robbed, and mugged; endure the abuse of those who have been ripped off. . . .
> [C]atching criminals is hard work, and it is dangerous work, too, and there is no fun in doing all that work, and exhausting yourself, only to see the bastard get off because you forgot one or two of the magic phrases that the Supreme Court says you have to recite over him before you put him in the cell.[22]

Cops react like everyone else to setback and frustration. Repeated failures by the courts to convict guilty pushers, robbers, and rapists tempt them to cheat and cut corners. Like the eponym of *The Judgment of Deke Hunter*, they may also lash out at a prosecutor, whose supposed botching of solid evidence sets a crook free. A trooper in *Kennedy for the Defense* (1980) obsesses so much over his failure to nail a car thief that he eats the driver's license and the registration of both the thief *and* his wife in order to bring charges against him. Other instances of police misconduct in Higgins aren't funny. In *The Rat on Fire*, a high-ranking cop commits arson; cops are accused of bribery and also of both planting evidence and beating up suspects in *Outlaws* (1987); in *Impostors* (1986), the police shut down a murder investigation for political reasons. Their malfeasance isn't unusual. Politics undermines both police morale and efficiency throughout the Higgins canon, preference and influence, and not merit, often dictating the doling out of assignments and promotions. In *Deke Hunter* and *Bomber's Law*, adultery dictates two out-of-town transfers.

Cynicism, careerism, and opportunism smudge the legal process at all levels, Higgins agreeing in principle with the proposition voiced at the start of William Gaddis's law-themed 1994 novel, *A Frolic of His Own*: "Justice? —You get justice in the next world, in this one you have the law."[23] Higgins packs his books with instances of lawyers tiptoeing through lists of technicalities to achieve justice. Lawyers *have* to walk with caution. The factual evidence that supports most legal briefs counts less than a jury's response to it. No shocks here; a good lawyer has to predict juries' reactions to what they've been told. And because juries are as *un*predictable as theater audiences, a good sense of both timing and group psychology rates high in litigation. Calling jurors "a bunch of nitwits" in *Sandra Nichols Found Dead*, Jerry Kennedy looks for ways "to bamboozle them, if the facts are against your client, as in criminal cases they generally are."[24]

Higgins takes this cynicism in stride. Attorneys must try to gain their client a favorable verdict, even if it means bending the law. But this truth also applies to opposing counsel, which can lead to some wild courtroom antics. Judges can be whimsical, too. Thus Jerry Kennedy, fully understanding the constraints he works within, rests content with the half-victory he gains at the end of *Sandra Nichols*. In his bittersweet last-chapter assessment of the trial that tops off the novel's action, he says, "That was never my job, to make what was wrong right. My job was the same one that I've always done. I figure near three million bucks" (SNFD 240). The outcome of the trial falls short of justice. But the freedom that Sandra's murderer finagled for himself cost a fortune by any standards. What's more, the murderer dug into his exchequer for a good cause. The three million he'll pay in damages will secure the futures of Sandra's orphaned children. A lawyer for some thirty years, Jerry has learned how to temper his expectations.

An experienced legal clerk in the late *Change of Gravity* (1997) takes the same balanced view of the law. "[T]here have been times in this courthouse when I think I may've done some good," muses Ambrose Merriman, adding, "maybe I've managed to actually grab some kid . . . and help him pull himself out of the mud. Give him a break, maybe the first one he's had." He says too that if he has managed to rescue a life a year that might have otherwise gone wrong during his eighteen years as a court officer, he'd sleep well.[25] He's wise to avoid asking how these hypothetical eighteen down-and-outers used the lucky break he gave them. Moved by kindness and patience rather than revenge, the good-hearted Amby has bent the rules to help the needy. Perhaps he had best ignore the effects of his charity. Like Higgins, he doesn't ask much from people, particularly the skid-row losers whose lives consist of thirty-day prison terms. Such misery leads to capital crimes.

How to deter them? Is there a point where charity should stop? A judge with thirty-six years on the bench exclaims to Amby, "Holy shit. . . ! As long as I've been . . . hearing this stuff, day after day after day, I get so I think I've heard all of it. . . . And then something else comes along, it gets so you can't believe half of . . . the things people dream up to do" (CG 378). No wonder he's shocked. A woman has just shot her estranged husband in the hallway adjoining the judge's courtroom. The bullet that canted Ellsworth Ryan through the doors of Judge Leonard Cavanaugh's courtroom shows the judge, among other things, that life is more volatile than he had imagined. Litigants are supposed to show the judges in charge of their trials their best behavior and shiniest image. The slug that creased Ryan's gut also created a legal impasse. And, with it, a precedent? As Amby says, "It looks like business as usual, and it is, but nothing makes any sense" (CG 345). The law is shackled at the very time it should be taking steps. Because of the technicality that stops the cops who heard Mrs. Ryan fire her handgun from testifying, the court can't move against her. Litigation that's most needful must wait until a way is found to negotiate points of law framed to help the law's smooth, even-handed operation.

Still worse, the viler the crime, the more hamstrung the criminal justice system. So contagious is this cramp that Higgins features it throughout his writing career. The police may build a case against a thug and then offer him freedom if he snitches his chiefs. Thugs who have already done hard time, like Eddie Coyle and Jerry "Digger" Doherty, dread going back to the joint, even if their chiefs have promised to take care of their family while they're inside. On the other hand, informing on a mobster like McKeach of *End of Day* will traumatize the snitch. No witness protection program, facial remake, or New Zealand passport will save him. And while the mob is looking for him, they'll try to smoke him out of hiding by maiming and killing his loved ones.

Such tactics are off limits to members of the legal establishment. But this ban may not be the worst of it. If criminal lawsuits favor the defendants, the more level playing field provided by civil law hobbles everybody. Higgins finds evidence for this grim logic in Charles Dickens's *Bleak House*. This 1853 classic centers on a legal action, Jarndyce vs. Jarndyce, that drags on for so long that the fortune the litigants were fighting over got sucked up by legal fees. Higgins quotes the book in the opening pages of *On Writing* (18–24). He also mentions it in *Wonderful Years* (188), *Defending Billy Ryan* (27) and *Bomber's Law*.[26] It's alluded to again in *Swan Boats* (196), and Jerry Kennedy refers to Jarndyce vs. Jarndyce in *Sandra Nichols* to voice his reluctance to argue a case so troublesome that it doesn't deserve his efforts (3).

Keeping Dickens center stage, we can add that these references fuel our faith in the claim of Mr. Bumble of *Oliver Twist* (1836) that the law is an ass. But unfortunately it's also the last line of civilized defense, after the failure of love, friendship, and decency, between us and the void. Though blind and sometimes asinine, it can still quiet our fears that our rights will be trampled; legal recourse fends off indigestion and the night sweats. A society without courts would also be one without laws. It would soon set all against all. The kangaroo trials of the Soviet Union and its satellites during the Cold War shamed the Kremlin in the court of world opinion. This lesson from history alone obliges any legal system to apply the law and dispense justice as fairly as possible.

This onerous job pivots on the lawyer-client relationship. The ideal client, all attorneys agree, obeys his lawyer, pays his legal bill quickly, and, putting his trust in the confidentiality of the lawyer-client privilege, offers full disclosure of what he knows about the issues under dispute. These three requirements often mesh; the lawyer of a balky client will usually need the help of a collection agency to get paid. What's more likely is that the client will hamstring his lawyer during trial and thus connive at his own conviction, as does James Walker in chapter 10 of *Outlaws*. The reason is clear; a defendant who lies to or holds back from counsel will probably also rile the jury by acting like his own lawyer. Nothing hurts defense counsel more than being ignorant of the essentials of the case he's working on than a client who represents himself.

On the other hand, a lawyer who wins his client's confidence can use the client-attorney privilege to build a strong case. A cooperative client, that is, one who trusts his lawyer to keep his words a secret, will volunteer information freely. Some of it, he may discover, will, in the hands of his skilled attorney, help him more than he had imagined. The treasure he offers might not have otherwise come forth, since attorneys often don't know enough about the cases they're trying to dig out the most vital information. For one thing, they lack the full historical record. For another, they have other clients. Although their attention can stay fixed during a trial, it drops soon afterward. Even the sharpest, most committed trial lawyers forget cases minutes after trial; they have to get ready for their next ones.

A judge's involvement can run still lower. A distracted judge in *Deke Hunter* rates his comfort and ease above justice. While hearing and pronouncing on evidence, he may also be worrying if the case under litigation could sidetrack the family vacation in Nantucket he had planned (CG 40). The vacation plans of a Judge Macarthur dictate the flow of the trial depicted in the book's next-to-last chapter; this is why he permits the prosecutor to lead the witness "a little" (CG 248) more than due process normally permits. The human factor can foil justice in different ways. In *Penance for Jerry Kennedy*, the title figure dreads facing "a judge in a bad mood" (5). He also learns in this same book that a vindictive judge can punish him by permitting opposing counsel to confuse and frustrate a witness. A judge may even body-slam a witness or litigant himself (PJK 13).

Some of this combativeness is natural. Lawyers motivated by a sense of fair play also like to win. In Boston, this urge takes its own form. Speaking of Washington, D.C., his hometown, a lawyer in *Edgar* calls the law a "generally local sport."[27] Conditions in Boston, where many more of Higgins's lawyers grew up and got schooled than in Washington, D.C., differ. One example, William Bulger, holder of the "Triple Eagle," namely, a Bachelor's, Master's, and law degree from Boston College, who later rose to the presidency of the University of Massachusetts, is the brother of the notorious thug James "Whitey" Bulger, the model for Arthur McKeach in Higgins's *End of Day*. Carrying matters forward, the legal trade in Higgins's Boston-based fiction both looks and acts like a closed system dogged by entropy; even the best families and most venerated firms fear that a Whitey Bulger could pounce at any time. This idea, prominent in the work of William Gaddis, explains why the intimacy and warmth of Boston's legal set in *Defending Billy Ryan* becomes so stifling it threatens to implode.

Entropy works in different ways. Jerry Kennedy's law practice has been languishing in this 1992 novel, unlike that of his ex-law school chum, Colin Ryan, Associate Justice of the Great Trial Court of Massachusetts. But in one of those inversions bred by closed systems, Judge Ryan needs Jerry's help. The judge's seventy-year-old father, Billy, veteran Commissioner of Public Works, faces jail time. He has been indicted for acting from motives of personal gain, that is, routing the construction of a new four-lane road through his own property. Naturally, the road deal boosted the value of Billy's property, earning him a potentially fat profit. Jerry's job: to find a technicality he can use to acquit his guilty client. But Billy won't cooperate. Jerry is stonewalled. The discovery that Billy is holding back information that could strengthen his defense prompts Jerry to lean on him. The next thing that happens is that the judge scolds Jerry for bullyragging his elderly father.

Higgins joins edge to middle again in *A Change of Gravity* to provide fresh slants on Boston's legal system. But now the reference point is the bedroom. One of the lawyers involved in the hearing described in the book's last chapter represented the presiding judge in her divorce suit several years earlier. He now represents Ambrose Merrion, former personal aide to Danny Hilliard, ex-chairman of Ways and Means in the Massachusetts House of Representatives *and* a former lover of the judge. Any ruling Barrie Foote makes against Amby will send her ex-lover to jail. The action ends before she pronounces. But it's implied, said Higgins in a posthumously published interview, that the decent, kindly Judge Foote will give Amby a pass.[28]

Others sitting on the bench act humanely, too. A judge in *Outlaws* who values civic duty thanks his jury for serving "at considerable cost and inconvenience." Two chapters hence, a different judge gives a pep talk to a jury without sugarcoating their ordeals.[29] The human side of jury duty stays to the fore. In *Outlaws* and elsewhere, judges will look out for their jurors' welfare, providing food and break time. They're showing wisdom. Often away from their jobs and homes for weeks on end, jurors can't let their collective ache to resume their normal routines distract them from the case they're hearing and must pronounce on.

For their work demands their full attention, if they're to give defendants, in the words of Supreme Court Justice Benjamin Cardozo (1870–1938), "fair trials, not perfect ones" (O 109). Note the qualification. Perfection isn't a human attribute, and its attainment in the courtroom or elsewhere is impossible. Discussing a client early in *Defending Billy Ryan*, Jerry Kennedy says, "Maybe he will be telling you the truth. Maybe I am not [telling the truth myself]. I think I am, but what do I know? Less and less as I go on" (1). Jerry is applying to the law the modernist belief that reality is too tricky and multiform to know, an opinion endorsed by a prominent lawyer who says of himself in *Wonderful Years*, "You've been practicing law for almost forty years and you still . . . wonder if you've done anything right" (162). This apologia reduces most legal verdicts to informed guesswork. Perhaps Higgins's admiration of Graham Greene[30] can shed light on this relativism. Even though Greene's Mexican priest in *The Power and the Glory* (1940) was a drunk and a fornicator, his risking his life to bring God to a poor village shows that life's most vital work sometimes belongs to the corrupt and the lowdown.

Voicing this humane argument in a different key is the hard-driving Fred Consolo of *Outlaws*. Seen first as a trooper, Consolo sweats and struggles to earn both a law degree and a lieutenant's bars. His ruthless self-discipline has also given him a passion for symmetry that denies living values. The squares and pentagons he draws (O 157) foretell the neat patterns that Maggie, the orphaned daughter of Sandra Nichols, razors into her flesh (SNFD 108). These marks are destructive. They even suggest a fascist mania for purity and order. This mania had worried Fred Consolo's mother (O 193). Better for all had he heeded her warning and given up his misguided quest for clarity and equilibrium. Life keeps derailing this quest. Fred is always right. But, because he defines things too closely, his rightness, or righteousness, has frozen his heart. His go-by-the-book rigor (a trait Higgins always deplores) cramps whatever workplace he's assigned to. Because he keeps faulting the efforts of his colleagues, no solid work gets done on his watch.

His rapid rise in law enforcement implies, in a variation of the Peter Principle, that he'll keep blocking production. Teamwork swamps individual effort in Higgins. In chapter 11 of *Deke Hunter*, which completes the book's halfway point, Deke warns his hockey-playing son, "Don't say you want to play defense and then go sneaking around, playing forward too" (104). If Sam charges the opponent's zone, he'll be out of position to defend his own. His misguided heroism could cost his team a goal. Analogously, "Cowboy Fred" (O 359) will frame unworkable plans and then blame everyone else when they fail.

Higgins may have tallied the damage caused by such freebooting in a 1978 talk, advisedly subtitled, "The Problem of Insubordination": "Our system of punishment . . . is a mess. Many know it. More do not. Until it is repaired, your job [i.e., professional criminal justicers] is to make it work as best it can."[31] With a Tolstoyan flourish, Higgins has put the best hopes of corrections officers in usage, consensus, and rule of thumb. Good will, common sense, training, and experience can serve justice better than a checklist of rules. Perhaps Higgins's Catholic upbringing explains his preference for the trial-and-error of tradition over cold, hard rules (his alter ego, or alter mind, Jerry Kennedy, talks about having grown up in a Catholic family, in Catholic schools, surrounded by Catholics [DBR 159]).

The car thief "Cadillac Teddy" Franklin, who's introduced in the first sentence of *Kennedy for the Defense*, Jerry's debut, suborns a witness in *Defending Billy Ryan* whose perjured testimony acquits Jerry's guilty client. Forget that Billy's acquittal doesn't quiet his grudge against Jerry. (And overlook, too, if you can, how Higgins smudged the finale of *Billy Ryan* by turning Cadillac Teddy into a deus ex machina). Billy's freedom rose from the muddle of his attorney's long, sometimes misguided dedication to a messy, but well-intended and useful, profession. Whereas adhering to the regs would have locked Billy up, the norms governing the muddle let the old rogue walk. And that's not so bad.

Notes

1. John Brady, "The Writer's Digest Interview: George V. Higgins," *Writer's Digest*, December 1975, 50.

2. John Williams, *Into the Badlands: Travels through Urban America* (London: HarperCollins), 200; Hugh M. Ruppersburg, "George V. Higgins," *Dictionary of Literary Biography*, 2 (1978), 236.

3. Ward Just, "Guns and Roses," *Boston Globe*, 19 December 2004, 3rd ed, 6(K); George V. Higgins, *On Writing* (New York, Henry Holt, 1990), 8; see also Erwin H. Ford, II, "Expiation Ritual in the Crime Novels of George V. Higgins, Ph. D. diss., State University of New York at Buffalo, 1988, 30-31.

4. George V. Higgins, *A Choice of Enemies* (New York: Knopf, 1984), 48; George V. Higgins, *Style vs. Substance: Boston, Kevin White, and the Politics of Illusion* (New York: Macmillan, 1984), 171; George V. Higgins, *Defending Billy Ryan* (New York: Henry Holt, 1992), 56; George V. Higgins, *Swan Boats at Four* (New York: Henry Holt, 1995), 87.

5. Ford, "Expiation Ritual," 9-10

6. William Vesterman, "Higgins's Trade," *Language and Style* 20 (1987), 229.

7. Williams, *Into the Badlands*, 206.

8. Higgins, *Style and Substance*, 170-1.

9. Elmore Leonard, "Introduction," George V. Higgins, *The Friends of Eddie Coyle* (1972; New York: Henry Holt/A John Macrae/Owl Book, 1995), vii.

10. George V. Higgins, "The Wrong Man?" *Memories: The Magazine of Then and Now* Spring, 1988, 69.

11. Higgins, *On Writing*, 177-93.

12. George V. Higgins, *The Progress of the Seasons: Forty Years of Baseball in Our Town* (New York: Henry Holt, 1989), 68.

13. George V. Higgins, *Trust* (New York: Henry Holt, 1989), 32.

14. George V. Higgins, *The Patriot Game* (New York: Knopf, 1982), 28.

15. Margaret Carlin, "Boston Brawler," *Rocky Mountain* [Denver] *News Sunday Magazine/Books* 27 July 1986, 23(M); see also Ford, 34, n.44.

16. George V. Higgins, *The Judgment of Deke Hunter* (Boston: Little, Brown: An Atlantic Monthly Press Book, 1976), 252.

17. George V. Higgins, *Impostors* (New York: Henry Holt, 1986), 154; George V. Higgins, *The Agent* (New York: Harcourt Brace), 17-8.

18. Matthew J. Bruccoli, "Editor's Note," George V. Higgins, *The Easiest Thing in the World* (New York: Carroll & Graf, 2004), ix.

19. Williams, *Into the Badlands*, 200.

20. George V. Higgins, *At End of Day* (New York: Harcourt, 2000), 20.

21. George V. Higgins, *Penance for Jerry Kennedy* (New York: Knopf, 1985), 104.

22. George V. Higgins, *The Friends of Richard Nixon* (Little Brown/An Atlantic Monthly Press Book, 1975), 5-6.

23. William Gaddis, *A Frolic of His Own* (New York: Poseidon, 1994), 11.

24. George V. Higgins, *Sandra Nichols Found Dead* (New York: Henry Holt/A John Macrae Book, 1997), 87, 85.

25. George V. Higgins, *A Change of Gravity* (New York: Henry Holt/A John Macrae Book, 1997), 29,30.

26. George V. Higgins, *Wonderful Years, Wonderful Years* (New York: Henry Holt, 1988), 188; George V. Higgins, *Bomber's Law* (Henry Holt/A John Macrae Book, 1993), 106.

27. George V. Higgins, *A Year or so with Edgar* (New York: Harper & Row, 1979), 46.

28. Pierre Bondil, facilitator, "Wonderful Times: Part Two," *C[rime] A[nd] D[etective] S[tories]*38, November 2000, 12.

29. George V. Higgins, *Outlaws* (New York: Henry Holt, 1987), 65, 91.

30. Brady, "Writer's Digest Interview," 52.

31. George V. Higgins, "Sentencing: The Problem of Individuation," *Trial: The National Legal Newsmagazine*, 14 (April, 1978), 44.

Chapter Two

Chasing Down the Mischief

Higgins is an original. He stands apart from the cult of abstraction and anomie. He also rejects the archetype of the lonely gumshoe whose moral code justifies getting beaten up and rejecting loose money or sex while operational. Nor does he conform to an American sensibility dominated by psychological realism, moral seriousness, or progressive politics. He says little about economic injustice, the destruction of the environment by global warming, or problems in health care caused by high unemployment. The perspective in his books is usually from the bottom up rather than, as in Dorothy L. Sayers, Ellery Queen, or P. D. James, from the top down.

He also faces the dark. Clay Tucker's 1987 review of *Outlaws* in the *Sunday Tennessean* begins, "The novel is an exercise in cynicism." Higgins seems to have made a practice of chilling southern hearts. Robert Merritt, writing in the Richmond *Times-Dispatch* in 1986 about the send-up of the media and the corrections establishment in *Impostors*, grumped, "He [Higgins] wants to show that unbridled ambition, greed, and lust are life's motivations, and that the system stinks."[1] Nor would Higgins have protested these groans from the South. He had already told John Brady that his books were "very black," and, even earlier, in a 1973 interview with Barbara A. Bannon, voiced a belief that most people are dishonest.[2] The gloom thickens. A policeman in *Outlaws* says, "Life sucks ands then you die" (34). Chapter 16 of *Defending Billy Ryan*, a novel whose painful subtext features adultery and pedophilia, ends with Jerry Kennedy saying the same thing (165). The statement recurs twice in dialogue in *Bomber's Law*, in chapter 9 (148) and then at the very end (286). A reference in *Outlaws* to "plain damned random sadness that we can't cure or prevent" (40) deepens the murk. Trouble will find us. There's more of it in the world than ease, and we feel it more keenly. Addressing this pessimism, Higgins referred in 1985 to his "Irish-Catholic upbringing of the Jansenist subspecies."

Perhaps Higgins's memory misled him here, even if he was thinking of the Jansenist demonizing of sex at the Irish seminary at Maynooth.[3] Carnality always counted less for Higgins than for Norman Mailer, John Updike, Philip Roth and the Catholic Flannery O'Connor. Cornelius Otto Jansen (1585–1638)

19

believed that only the converted, namely those exempted by God from punishment, receive divine grace. A Jansenist cross owned by a character in Graham Greene's *Third Man* (1950) shows Christ's arms raised to symbolize His having died for the converted alone. The converted are as scarce in Higgins as are those ravaged by lust. Yet Greene's belief, most famously portrayed in *The End of the Affair* (1951), that God's grace can resemble punishment, does strike a chord in *Wonderful Years* (1988), a work that both quotes Greene's book title (3) and ends with the words, "Everybody gets just about what they want. It's just that they don't recognize it. . . . It doesn't look the same as what they had in mind" (261).

The novel's action gives these words a Brechtian spin. One of its main figures, the gentle Eugene Arbuckle, went to jail after killing a man who had lured him into fighting. When he learned, while riding out his prison term, that his wife had found another man, he wished her luck; a young beauty can't stop living when her husband is doing time in the slammer. Bucky continues to extend charity to women who wronged him. Years later he responds to the news that his much-younger girlfriend has probably infected him with HIV by telling her that, by confronting the problem with their mutual love, they will solve it. His faith isn't misplaced. At times, the afflicted in *Wonderful Years* seem to touched, like some of those in Greene, by God's loving hand. The heel who made Sharon Stoddard HIV positive (and who had also been badgering Bucky) dies in a car crash; he can't hurt anyone now, and, contrary to expectations, might have even brought Sharon and Bucky closer together.

Troublemaking Steve Cole isn't the only one to die in the closing chapters of *Wonderful Years*. Higgins also records the death of the alcoholic manic-depressive Nell Farley. One of her husband's business associates had Nell in mind when he said in the book's first chapter, "Everybody's got their personal limit of shit, and then something happens, over the limit, and they crack" (8). Perhaps God gave Nell more shit than she could handle because, like the God sometimes intimated in Kafka, He valued her pain more than her happiness. This intimation chimes with Higgins's suggestion that Nell may have died in a state of grace.

But the theophany that pits a Jansenist yearning for transcendence against human frailty, as in Patrick White's *Aunt's Story* (1948) and Peter Shaffer's 1973 *Equus*, rarely occurs in Higgins. Though important, Nell Farley of *Wonderful Years* may be his only member of "the cult of sanctified sinners," as George Orwell called the beneficiaries of Greene's oddball view of salvation. Jerry Kennedy speaks of contrition, humility, and Christian compassion in *Penance*, which ends with his dismissing life's brevity and sorrow as "God . . . just having a few laughs" (199, 189, 321). Higgins hasn't pitted his characters against an implacable creator who laughs at their grief. He's only trying to add depths and recesses to Jerry's personality.

Rarely does Catholic dogma, ritual, or iconography figure in the Higgins novels. Catholicism is a given identity rather than a source of uplift, wisdom, or angst. It's more of a habit than a moral force or fever directed to those vast unseen presences on which life depends. Political boss Bernie Morgan of *A Choice of Enemies* (1984) makes the point when he tells a rival, "You can't hurt me with my people, and I haven't got yours behind me anyway; no matter if I turn into Jesus tomorrow and announce that every one of them is saved. They'll still vote against me" (CE 269). Bernie is speaking from a context he and his hearer recognize, respect, and set store by. His reference to Jesus comes as naturally to him as would some crowd-pleasing antics at a political rally.

But even if Higgins expects Protestants to attend this hypothetical rally, he doesn't replace the Lord of Hosts with the core of Protestant worship, namely, the individual's bond with God. Conscience hasn't swamped faith. The prevalence of lawyers in the fiction infers the dominance of the Protestant imperatives of duty, discipline, and self-denial in Higgins's work; even his crooks scramble to stay out of stir. But one would scour the canon in vain for examples of Max Weber's conflation of morality in trade with either a Calvinist trust in Scripture or an Evangelical emphasis upon plainness and simplicity. Religion is an absorbed, not an applied, presence, for Higgins. Even his priests drink and golf in private clubs.

This is not to say that his work withholds glimpses of transcendence. Moments of self-overcoming do brighten his people's lives. But Higgins's faith in the goodness or redeemability of human nature will take an existential form. In the character of Frank Macdonald, *Penance* features a power broker whose unresponsiveness to Jerry Kennedy's cries of help, after he gets Jerry into trouble, recalls the absent ruler in Shakespeare's *Measure for Measure* and the no-show God in Samuel Beckett's *Waiting for Godot* (1952) and John Fowles's *Collector* (1963), whose nonintervention fosters both coping power and growth in those who have stopped looking for divine help. A woman says at the end of chapter 12 of *Wonderful Years* that everybody living in the book's time frame is enacting "a pagan theology" in which "all the gods are dead" (136). Instead of waiting for God to solve their problems, they practice self-reliance. But whence this can-do Yankee virtue? Higgins wrote so much that he makes you feel that sooner or later everything will show up in his work; though presumably no animal-rights activists people his work, he describes in *Bomber's Law* the rigors of dog kenneling (249).

His lawyer's fondness for precision and economy inclines him to the principle of Occam's (or Ockham's) razor (e.g., DBR 44), which urges the stripping of any argument or thesis to its basic components. He'll brandish the razor in surprising ways. Either an extreme of rugged individualism or a yearning for oriental repose drives the aphorism, "Most of our troubles are directly attributable to our refusal to sit quietly in our rooms." The aphorism, credited to Descartes in *Style Versus Substance* (243) and, correctly, to Pascal in the short story, "The Last Wash of the Teapot," from *The Easiest Thing in the World* (268), ratifies the assurance with which Jay Quentin of *Impostors* and Gene Arbuckle of *Wonderful Years* can deflect blows that would crush most of their richer, more socially powerful counterparts. Happiness for both men stems from a refusal to cast blame. Higgins likes this idea. His epigraph to chapter 14 of *Style*

Versus Substance (1984), from Francis Bacon, "A man that studieth revenge keeps his own wounds green" (201), proclaims the wisdom of learning forgiveness, acceptance, and love. These virtues defuse negative energy and build good happy lives, attainments rare enough not only in Higgins but also in his literary heroes Greene, Hemingway, and John O'Hara.

I

Higgins's sensibility dovetails with novelistic convention. A strong believer in the primacy of social bonds, he embraces features of both the conservative and liberal temperaments. He clearly favors tolerance, but rejects the idea that crime is fundamentally benign, posing no threat to the fabric of society. He's not a comforting writer. The dim view he takes of our capacity for self-improvement and self-knowledge explains his attraction to crime. No environment is crime safe. In *Eddie Coyle*, a felon returns home from jail to a wife who, in his absence, became a Jehovah's Witness. Her fanaticism drives him back to the slammer; rather than coming home to her pieties at night, he reverts to crime. He might have gone straight, too. Higgins sees good and bad commingling in both people and human affairs. A priest in *Victories* says of a young battlefield casualty who made some bad mistakes, "He wasn't a really bad kid. But he was not a really good kid, either."[4] *Nobody*'s hands are clean. Young Anthony French's misdeeds killed him. He could have avoided death by crawling across a Vietnamese field, as he was trained to do, rather than standing up in it. He'd have been spared a trip to Vietnam altogether had his civilian wrongdoing in Vermont not peaked in an army enlistment.

The stain spread. The efforts of Hank Briggs, an ex-major leaguer who scores a political upset at novel's end, sparked a chain of events that sent Anthony to Vietnam. Other factors, most of them beyond Anthony's control, sped his downfall. Erwin H. Ford's reference to the "sense of vast pity and sorrow for weakness" he saw permeating *Wonderful Years*[5] applies here, as well. If up-country Anthony French were more decent and wholesome, he'd qualify as a tragic hero in the A. E. Housman vein. Higgins's people walk close to chaos much of the time, and the most casual flub can devastate them. Perhaps Jay Quentin and Gene Arbuckle had it right; forgive those who have wronged you, shake off hardship, and hope for the best. We all abut a calamity that's waiting to snatch us. But, as is implied by Hank Briggs's election-victory speech, a fusion of baseball and political rhetoric, it hasn't engulfed the whole human landscape.

The calamity can also be fended off. Higgins sets forth a Tolstoyan view of history that fuses loss and gain alongside winners and losers. Split has yielded to spectrum. Both in victory and defeat, everybody takes part. Participation is key, for it presumes belief in a cause that deserves effort, and, often, sacrifice. In any joint project, it's sometimes hard to say who gave up more, whose efforts counted the most, and whose loyalty ran deepest. Perhaps posterity will decide. Those involved in the struggle lack both the information and the perspective to judge. Germane to the point is this Hamlet-like sentiment voiced by a lawyer in *Wonderful Years*: "How little we know. . . . How little we dream of, in our daily lives, what's going on all around us" (116). Yet not only must we live in ignorance; we must also judge and take sides, even while we're still working out the parameters of victory and defeat. New representative-elect for his district in Vermont Hank Briggs conflates these conundra into a matter of presence and absence, that is, who was there at the time. The only certainty on the baseball diamond or the battlefield is the identity of those who took part:

> Okay, that's the way the systems work. Someone has to get the credit, someone has to take the blame. But the reality's different. The other guys on the team had just as much or more to do with getting us a win as I had more or less to do with us taking a loss in the games where the other teams won. So how many victories are there in a game or an election? Probably, I think, as many as there are people who took part. So who knows what victories really are, then? What they mean, if they mean anything? The only thing that matters is that we were all there when it happened. (298)

This rebuttal of the great man theory of history invites another Tolstoyan echo, from Higgins's "Last Wash of the Teapot." The story's narrator, a Harvard Law School graduate in his fifties, says near the end, "The only thing you ever learn is that you don't know anything" (Easiest 277). This statement is no nihilistic shrug. Rather than caving in to moral defeatism, the speaker is referring to the pitfalls of passing judgment. Ignorance in his sense of the word combines mental clarity with the moral courage to resist peer pressure. It's an ability to weigh both sides of an issue fairly. Higgins respects it. "F. Scott Fitzgerald . . . said that the first-rate mind is one enabling its possessor to hold two contradictory ideas at the same time," he wrote in *The Progress of the Seasons* (203). It recurs verbatim, Keatsian subtext and all, in *On Writing* (92). A posthumously published interview in *Crime and Detective Stories*, or *CADS*, shows how Higgins's disdain for absolutes helped him write what's perhaps his funniest scene, a brawl between a husband and wife in *The Rat on Fire* (1981), a feat he managed, moreover, without worrying subtleties and distinctions (CADS 2, 6). Edward L. Galligan's obituary in *Sewanee Review* hails this open-mindedness when it cites Higgins's "complex and human" treatment of "social and political issues."[6]

Higgins's fine sense of that which can't be measured or calculated, but only felt, colors his work ethic. His career as a criminal lawyer taught him that a bank robber would probably lie to his attorney in a heartbeat. But a client who defies counsel, like Harry Mapes of *Penance* (1985), could also sink his own case. Better to heed the training and experience of a pro. A lawyer in *Wonderful Years* says that he'd never tell a barber how to cut hair. Hank Briggs buys the welfare of his wife and kids by investing his money with a financial expert. His pitching career taught him that the same teamwork that wins ball games applies everywhere. Not only his success but also his well-being has hinged on his accepting the interdependency fostered by the team concept: "If I knew anything about handling money, I wouldn't have played ball. If the guy that handles my money knew anything about baseball, he'd be doing that" (V 35).

The cultivation of expertise helps all. By sticking to what they know, both the baseballer and the financial wonk focus their skills. They also learn to respect the materials of their crafts. The words of a superintendent of an apartment building in *Change of Gravity* neglected by its owners convey the rewards of solid workmanship. A sturdy building requires less care than a dump; efficiently running pumps won't flood the basement, just as well-insulated wiring is less likely to short out and high-quality oil burners remain a good bet to transmit heat (CG 404–6). Higgins's respect for good materials and workmanship also comes forth in *A Choice of Enemies* and *The Mandeville Talent* (1991), where shoddiness in building and road construction always brings confusion, disorder, and extra unwanted expense. Don't cheat, Higgins is saying. Cheapjack materials used carelessly by poorly trained hands result in flimsy, shaky work that will come apart quickly. The other side of the argument, which Jerry Kennedy's legman "Bad-eye" Mulvey favors, comes straight from Adam Smith. Good work done for a fair wage feeds the worker's self-esteem. It also boosts business; a pleased customer is more likely to return than one who feels cheated (KD 179–82). Viewed in the larger picture, high-quality goods and services stimulate business while also sparking a good balance of trade and high levels of employment. Economic health comes from robust competition, not naked self-interest.

Quality control matters to contractor Vinnie Mahoney of *Choice* because he knows that happy customers don't merely come back; they also recommend him to their friends and colleagues. But more is at stake for Vinnie than growing a business. He takes pride in his work; anything less than a first-rate job goes back to the shop (CE 116). Higgins admires Vinnie's high standards. He also knows that they depend upon years of hard work as well as natural skills. Any job deserves this commitment. An expert in speedboat engines in *Kennedy for the Defense* and a crack-shot restorer of vintage cars in *Sandra Nichols Found Dead* comprise a mini-elite. But the elite's avatar isn't a fictional character, even though he's mentioned in at least eight of the Higgins books.[7] He's the Hall of Fame defenseman for the Boston Bruins, Bobby Orr. Nearly all of Higgins's references to him occur advisedly in dialogue. So outstanding was his hockey game that he quickly comes to mind when Bostonians of all stripes are looking for a standard of excellence.

A book like *Impostors* will channel this worth into the trickery, greed, and hustling that feed our national heritage. Except for William Gaddis's *JR* (1975), the novelistic treatment of predatory capitalism in Higgins could set new limits for sardonic comedy. The adroit, coolheaded players in Higgins who enjoy the most success rarely amount to more than the sum of grungy motives and opportunism despite the tasseled Guccis they wear to the office. To get the attention of her fast-cooling lover Mark Baldwin, Sylvia Francis of *Impostors* has been shoplifting wares she could easily afford to buy. Now that her desperation has driven her to attempt suicide, the media giant Baldwin decides to dispose of her, agreeing with his lawyer that "sooner's better than later" (I 232). After establishing plausible deniability, he sets up Sylvia's death. Then this paragon of expediency, untrammeled by Karamazov guilt, moves on with his life.

His heartlessness invokes Freud's calling love and work the cornerstones of our humanness. Work in Higgins is desperate and coercive, and love usually falls short and leaves scars. Sylvia Francis died because she disrupted the balance of Mark Baldwin's sexual and business arrangements. Her pain can't be subsumed within a larger, encompassing equilibrium. As its many anomalies prove, her competitive society is no benign self-regulating system. Higgins deliberately gives her a gay husband and makes Baldwin a divorcé who still sleeps with his wife. But to what effect? Do these arrangements strip from the institution of the family the benevolence of a loving God? The family in Higgins often flags and founders. Married in *Kennedy for the Defense*, (1980), the first installment of the Jerry Kennedy quartet, Jerry will lose his wife to her job and a fellow realtor; a daughter he had a loving relationship with in *Defense* quarrels with him in *Penance* (1985); by *Sandra Nichols*, the final Kennedy book, she has moved to Colorado without a degree but with a husband Jerry has always loathed, and the two kids she had with him aren't even named.

This novel, which describes casual sex, betrayal, and murder within the family, also finds Jerry so fallen that he's left out of the book's title for the first time in the series. He also belongs to a nominally pluralist democracy that has disenfranchised millions of blacks and helped overthrow at least nine democratically elected governments in Latin America. He no more embodies the American dream than Fitzgerald's Gatsby or Arthur Miller's Willie Loman. None of these men gets what he wants; instead, all of them make us ask whether *what* they wanted was worth having, to begin with.

Jerry's puzzlement floods the canon. Higgins is a lucid, pitiless observer of both the nature and the deployment of power. Politics and crime interface in his work in a tough, ruthless environment. The opening pages of *Bomber's Law* (1993) describe two cops on a stakeout. The cops, an older Irishman and a younger Italian-American, lend insight into a Boston built largely around social-professional bonds whose building blocks include jokes and hierarchies. The system conjured up by the barbed joshing of Bob Brennan and Harry Dell'Appa also includes ambivalence and danger. Higgins depicts the awkwardness and instability of male friendships—the aggressiveness informing male banter and the spite that erupts when success divides colleagues, lifetime friends, and brothers. Dell'Appa has attained the same rank, namely, Sergeant, as his former mentor. Some twenty years that ex-mentor's junior, he also has different, more up-to-date, ideas about law enforcement. Nor has Brennan's impending retirement cooled his resentment of Dell'Appa. And it will keep simmering in the tense, cramped atmosphere Higgins has induced by seating the men alongside each other in a parked car for an hour or more.

The car, though motionless, has veered into a realm rife with casualties, the dirt and danger of power politics. A passage in *A Year or So with Edgar* (1979) defines politics thus: "You reward your friends, and you punish your enemies" (45). This grim lesson, dramatized by the novel Higgins would publish five years hence, *A Choice of Enemies*, galvanizes the following adage from *Victories*: "Politics is a choice of enemies. You're gonna get it up the ass, matter what you do" (73). The following statement by the same veteran pol, Vermont's Speaker of the House, sharpens his adage: "[T]here isn't any difference between shit and politics, except that no sane human being would ever step in either one if he had a choice" (75).

The squalor and filth of politics always taints the virtues. The real-life Henry Peterson, "stuffed to the gills with integrity" (FRN 33), was betrayed by his bosses during the Watergate break-ins. Playing it straight also brings Higgins's Robert Wainwright of *Victories* to grief. The virtues this banker's son shares with his fellow Vermonters—reticence, loyalty to tradition, and decency—got him elected to Congress fourteen times. His constituents particularly admire the thrift of this stoical Republican. A congressman who returns to the Treasury 30–40 percent of his annual office budget will vex his staffers, but he'll gladden the members of his tax-minded voting base. The voters in his district keep re-electing him because they know that, by nixing all sorts of social reform programs (which would only help remote urbanites, anyway), he's protecting *them*. They prize this stewardship. Another politician in *Victories* loses an election because his belief that the poor shouldn't lose their homes to buy medicine entails a tax hike. A Bob Wainwright will torch this candidate at the polls every time—unless the unforeseen intrudes. The upright Wainwright is also uptight. Late in *Victories*, he spurns information that could sink his foe because he disclaims the smear tactics he'd have to use to go public with it. He runs clean campaigns, even if it means ending his political career.

Unlike him, most pols learn before reaching eighty the importance of flexibility and compromise. Unfortunately, few of them know how far they can bend the rules without breaking them. This is one of the "moral dilemmas" that, Higgins claims, drives his fiction.[8] And they vex everybody—policemen and building superintendents, businessmen and homemakers, as well as politicians. How to steer through them? A smart reasoned assessment of one's chances entails knowing when to stop, not asking for too much, and avoiding the quick fix. A police inspector in *Outlaws*, scornful of the report submitted by a lazy coroner, says, "the simplest, easiest explanation's always the one that stupid . . . bastard picks" (37). Later in the book, a DA, supposedly quoting H. L. Mencken, says in heat, "For every complex problem there is almost invariably a simple explanation—that's almost invariably wrong" (193). But right answers can elude the diligent, too. Higgins, both a lawyer trained in the art of negotiation and a novelist who looks at the emotional reverberations of issues, often sounds baffled himself. The sentence, "He that increaseth wisdom . . . increaseth sorrow," appears in *Bomber's Law* (259) and then twice in the short story collection, *The Easiest Thing in the World* (95, 177). Was the later Higgins framing a scenario featuring elders who, like some Old Testament patriarchs, suffer as they age? Elders who even lack the consolation of happy childhoods they can recall?

II

Higgins's dialogue-driven novels transcend dramatic event. They also consider why events happen and how they touch those who partake of them, that is, what the events mean. The path to this rich thematic vein bypasses the dreary deconstructive and puritanical strongholds of the politically correct. But dreariness can't be altogether shunned. Power in postwar America has shifted to unelected party bosses, lawyers, industrial magnates, and union apparatchiks, namely, people of limited accountability. Trouble also lies behind doors of opportunity that have been admitting minorities in recent decades. The operations chief of a multimillion-dollar sports agency in *The Agent* is black, and *Defending Billy Ryan* and *Change of Gravity* both include black judges. But these success stories are trifles. White America's scramble for profit and power, which crushed hundreds of thousands of Africans, is still thriving in Boston. And it could smash Boston's white population, too. Underlying Robert Campbell's *Washington Post* review of *Trust* is the belief that the Augustinian doctrine of original sin and total depravity Higgins learned in parochial school also chilled his heart. The characters in *Trust*, Campbell argues, "have no loyalty to one another and nothing more than passing twinges of compassion. Instead, they have angles, hidden agendas, game plans, self-serving strategies and a deep, abiding love for money."[9]

Boston's underworld, which claims many of Higgins's characters, is a distinct culture with a set of customs, mores, and rites that it uses to enforce its rules. Disciplined and organized, it also has a corporate sensibility: maximize profits, and come down hard on all who break its laws—with some exceptions; killing journalists and cops hurts business. Higgins conveys the force of the codes governing organized crime by giving his gangsters some excellent arguing positions. Indeed, his antagonists can out-argue his heroes (e.g., O 152). (Think too of the Artful Dodger's "this ain't the shop for justice" speech in *Oliver Twist* and the persuasiveness of Deputy Governor Thomas Danforth in Arthur Miller's *Crucible* [1953]). We want the good guy to win, but also credit his opponent's point of view. Higgins writes about gangsters, some of whom are paranoid, violent, and racist. Yet he also engenders sympathy as well as revulsion for them, repeat offenders who have done hard time. Unlike the Victor Hugo's Jean Valjean in *Les Miserables* and Vittorio de Sica's bicycle thief (1949), they weren't urged into crime by a sudden hardship.

Higgins has tapped into their psyches—and ours. We tend to like rascals like Eddie Coyle, he knows, because we privately suspect that what they have fled—monogamy, respectability, and the hierarchies of the workplace—is, in fact, a raw deal. The aggressive, amoral rhythms of the urban industrial state block the drive to get ahead. It may happen on a busy street near Boston's Common (*Eddie Coyle*), at a Red Sox game (*Impostors*), or at Coldstream, the dog track near Boston where Sgt. Harry Dell'Appa meets the professional hit man, Joe Mossi, in *Bomber's Law*. Higgins's docudrama treatment of such scenes mixes fact and fiction so deftly that we have no idea what will happen next and whether it's true or not. The brew reads like a Pirandellian puzzle. Where does fiction intersect with life? we wonder. At what point do the characters take on a life of their own? Finally, how does this life affect ours? The hoods and lawmen who josh over drinks might also threaten our safety. But we can't be sure how it will happen.

That's the way Higgins wants it. In an unpublished essay called "Dances with Muses," housed at the Higgins Archive in the Thomas Cooper Library of the University of South Carolina–Columbia, he said, "When I tell novels, I ask a good deal of my readers." Not only does he retreat from the page to let the reader decipher the characters' motives. The deep structure of all of his books also disclaims any moralizing that may have accidentally seeped in. For instance, Higgins owned a sailing vessel called *Scribbler*, which he's seen piloting on the dust jacket of *Swan Boats* (1995). The first chapter of *Dreamland* (1977) shows Andrew Collier, one of Higgins's vilest characters, steering a fishing boat, an act that foreshadows his urge to run people's lives, which he does whenever he sees a chance to do harm.

Nautical references like "cleating the line down"[10] throng this novel that ends with some scandalous revelations and, if Higgins can be trusted, the madness of its narrator (CADS 2, 38). Sorrow and sailing mingle again in *Kennedy for the Defense* (1980). Catastrophe topples a sea-craft mechanic (21), and the older man who meets Jerry's college-age daughter at a lakefront lodge, Jerry fears, may have also fucked her. Further evidence of Higgins's adoption of Flaubert's equation of water and death comes forth in *Swan Boats*, a novel that features a "damned third-rate mural" (194) depicting pleasure boats. Despite its mediocrity, the faded mural evokes *Bleak House* as well as *Madame Bovary*; its maintenance, to avoid a lawsuit, surpasses by far its intrinsic worth. The problems the mural have already caused emerge in a novel, whose main action, the undoing of bank director David Carroll, develops on a ship that's crossing the Atlantic Ocean.

Higgins knew and loved cars more than he did sailing crafts. The title page of his undergraduate story, "No Traveler Returns," is splashed with the insignia of a Jaguar XK 150.[11] He continued to dote on expensive foreign cars. "Introduction," his unpublished essay about his troubles with the IRS, tells how he drove a Jaguar XKE convertible and a Porsche 911 in the 1970s (5). The repair and restoration of these cars can move to the fore of the novels. An expert in retrofitting European classic cars (and such is Higgins's own expertise on the topic that he knows that the prewar Jaguar was called a Swallow Sport [SNFD 146]) plays a vital part in *Sandra Nichols*, just as major characters in *Trust* and *Change of Gravity* sell cars for a living.

Higgins's car fetish declares itself in different ways. In *Cogan's Trade* (1974), cars with or without their drivers appear at the start of several chapters.[12] The book even matches cars to their owners. A gangster compares driving a Chrysler 300F at 80 mph to having sex with a beautiful woman. Later, Jackie Cogan, a professional hit man whose tweed jacket shows his skill in the art of concealment, will drive a Plymouth Duster (211), an economy coupe more expensive than the Ford Pinto that appealed to younger drivers with families. This detail was researched. Higgins's pairing of motorists to cars indicates, along with the motorists' socioeconomic levels, the images the motorists *want* to project. In *Eddie Coyle*, an aide of a Mafia don important enough to deliver the don's messages personally drives a silver Lincoln Continental, a town car luxury sedan (160).

A district may also be defined by the vehicles that pass along its streets. Thus the Ford Country Squires and Volvo station wagons seen in Framingham, Massachusetts, bespeak "a nice neighborhood" (PJK 130) inhabited by fewer singles than families, including soccer moms. Higgins takes his practice of matching cars to the class game full circle in *Bomber's Law* and *End of Day*. These late novels feature super-hoods whose dusty old gray Cadillacs affirm the haughty self-rule of their drivers; neither Short Joe Mossi nor McKeach worries about his image.

Higgins's most brilliant tour de force writing on the subject appears in *Trust*, a book full of references to automobile construction, maintenance, and repair along with the marketing of cars. This automotive lore sorts well in a novel parts of which unfolds in car dealerships. In chapter 10 of Higgins's 1989 work, the car salesman Earl Beale uses superb sales technique on a young woman who has come to the lot to buy her first car, laughing, listening patiently, withholding information, and putting the information he does include in the glossiest light. And if the gentle, low-key approach he uses with Charlene Gaffney and her mother includes some lies to lower sales resistance, it serves the same goals as the rest of his sales pitch. When later asked by a colleague the goal of his elaborate spiel, he answers, "Only what they wanted done" (T 109). He's right. The two women entered the showroom to buy a car.

And buy a car they do, even if it's not the one they looked at and test drove in chapter 10. Earl's next customer is a man. Adding another measure of balance, Michael Forest has come to the dealership to *sell* a car, not buy one. Predictably enough, Earl projects a different persona to him than he did to the women who just left his lot. Though Earl laughs with him, he's also more direct without being rude and, striving to lower the purchase price of Forest's car, displays a wide range of automotive savvy. The coerciveness of solid information replaces charm and tact; he's the expert now, citing the Ford Crown Victoria's fouled plugs, cheap shocks, and scuffed, bottom-of-the-line tires (115). But Earl's true professionalism shows in his manual inspection of the 1955 Ford. This mastery gains emphasis from parallel phrasing that conveys the careful attention he bestows upon the many details of his task. In a superb marriage of knowledge and technique, Charlene will buy the car that Earl white-gloves—but without Earl's recording the sale in his employer's ledger book:

> After a while he [Earl] went into the lot and walked around the car, running the tips of his fingers along the rim strips, stooping to rap his knuckles lightly on the liners inside the wheel wells, noting the fit of the removable skirt over the right wheel, placing his hands on the trunk and then on the hood to jounce the car on its springs, touching the treads of the tires, opening the driver's side door and examining the jambs and sills, getting in and looking at the odometer reading. (T 112)

No sooner does Higgins compel our admiration for Earl's expertise than he challenges it. In chapter 14, a local pol says of him, "Earl is trouble, and what comes from Earl is trouble" (165). The pol speaks home. The ex-con Earl Beale may have even acquired automotive know-how so he could corrupt it. In chapter 1, a trooper stops him for speeding in a car owned by his girlfriend, one Mary P. Slate (5). Intriguingly, Ed Cobb, who will call Earl "trouble" (165) and then "a rat" who "never did a decent thing for anyone" (V 67), also says that Hank Briggs's status as a political outsider or "blank slate" (V 217) could help him win an upcoming election. The reference to John Locke's tabula rasa is apt in both cases. Hank's nonexistent political record does help him get elected, and the marks experience has cut into Earl deepen his moral darkness.

Earl keeps outsmarting himself. In chapter 2 of *Trust* he's told to drive a Mercedes 190SL that was used in a lover's tryst to the crusher. But instead of doing that, he sells it. What follows is a chain of developments that slot into place so neatly that they describe a self-regulating deistic world. Everything tallies. The car hosts another lovers' tryst. And it will resurface at the end of Higgins's next novel, *Victories*, as will Earl, but only as a voice on the telephone out of hearing distance. That voice makes an ugly offer that's turned down. The rejection and fading away of Earl are both thematic. An expert in cars who both misuses and steals them, he fuels the idea that anyone who shares Higgins's passions comes to grief. The idea can be supported. Cars in Higgins often emit auras of danger and death. Men get shot to death in cars in *Eddie Coyle* and *Cogan's Trade*. Another is killed by a drunken driver in the last chapter of *Wonderful Years*. Nor are women safe from car death. Two of them die in a crash in the short work, "An Interview with Diane Fox,"[13] along with others in *Impostors* and *Change of Gravity*. These catastrophes have a common source. Higgins discussed his car fetish, calling it "virulent and pathological." Problems with "front ends, wheel bearings, distributors . . . and [the] clutches"[14] of fancy sports cars he owned as a student ate up all of his, and also a good deal of his father's, money. But he continued to buy and drive foreign sports cars as an adult, scolding himself for the indulgence by portraying Peter Wade of *Sandra Nichols*, the canon's number one connoisseur of vintage cars, as totally vicious (82).

His other vices he could have done more to curb. Even though he stopped smoking, he continued to drink. The booze that shortened his life meant at least as much to him as his boats and cars. Higgins's treatment of it shows the same veiled self-disapproval. Bars and the products they sell unleash a contagion of ugliness. The main figure of "An Interview with Diane Fox" had alcohol in her blood when she died driving a car. Eddie Coyle was drunk when he was murdered by the bartender Dillon, whose own death is reported in *Cogan's Trade*. A prostitute's statement in *Trust*, "My father hasn't drawn a sober breath in all the years I've known him" (197), posits a tie between his drinking and *her* corruption. What befalls the senior law clerk, Larry Lane of *Change of Gravity*, sharp-focuses the tie. Forbidden his beloved alcohol at home, Lane dies alone with his bottle in a run-down apartment. The dangers that occur in the presence of drink can also erupt suddenly, the most violent scene Higgins ever wrote exploding in a south Boston bar in chapter 20 of *The Patriot Game*.

Notes

1. Clay Tucker, "George Higgins Tale Skillful but Cynical," *Sunday Tennessean*, 11 October 1987, 7-F; Robert Merritt, "Writers Try to Break Away from Stereotypes," *Richmond Times-Dispatch*, 15 June 1986, F-5.

2. Brady, "Writer's Digest Interview," 27; Barbara A. Bannon, "Publisher's Weekly Interview: George V. Higgins," *PW*, 15 January 1973, 26.

3. George V. Higgins, "Professor Richardson et al.: A New England Education," *New England Journal of Public Policy*, 1 (Summer-Fall 1985): 43; Warren Coffey, "Flannery O'Connor," *Commentary* 40, 5 (November 1965): 93–9.

4. George V. Higgins, *Victories* (New York: Henry Holt/A John Macrae Book, 1990), 272.

5. Erwin H. Ford, "Higgins Adds New Touches of Humanity," *Buffalo News*, 4 December 1988, E-13.

6. Edward L. Galligan, "George V. Higgins 1939–1999," *Sewanee Review*, CVIII (Winter 2000), 148.

7. Higgins, *Eddie Coyle* 175; *Richard Nixon* 227; *Progress*, 10, 78; *Style Versus Substance*, 12; *Penance*, 109; *Bomber's Law*, 214; George V. Higgins, *Kennedy for the Defense* (New York: Knopf, 1980), 144.

8. Brian Doyle, "My Lunch with George," *Boston College Magazine* 50 (Spring 1991): 25.

9. Robert Campbell, "A Perfect Sales Pitch," *Washington Post*, 22 October 1989, X5.

10. George V. Higgins, *Dreamland* (Boston: Little, Brown/An Atlantic Monthly Press Book, 1975), 95.

11. George V. Higgins, "No Traveler Returns," *Stylus: The University Quarterly of Boston College* 73 (November 1959): 44.

12. George V. Higgins, *Cogan's Trade* (New York: Knopf, 1974), e.g., 59, 120.

13. George V. Higgins, "An Interview with Diane Fox," *Sewanee Review* CVII (Winter 1999): 7–17.

14. George V. Higgins, "Witness: Something of a Memoir," *Massachusetts Review* 10 (Summer 1969): 597, 602.

Chapter Three

The Guys onna Street and Others

Besides hitting the mark, Michael Putney's claim that Higgins's first novel, *The Friends of Eddie Coyle* (1972), was "a novel of manners,"[1] turned out to be prophetic. Throughout his career, Higgins wrote about standards of social behavior and interpersonal dynamics, often using the family as a reference point. It's fitting that Edward L. Galligan called his review of *Bomber's Law* "Henry James among the Cops in Boston."[2] He's on target. The Jamesian anti-hero who's missing from his life appears in *City on a Hill* (1975), *Dreamland* (1977), and *Swan Boats at Four* (1995). Also like James, Higgins often implies more than he expresses; a hood like Eddie Coyle who had his hand smashed for botching a crime needn't be warned of the dangers of crossing the mob. Higgins's occasional references to the Heisenberg Principle (e.g., V 258, BL 88), which argues that measuring any system also disrupts it, reflects a feel for nuances that imbues the fiction. For instance, in *End of Day*, his last novel, two big-time crooks act bored or pretend to be daydreaming when they hear some FBI agents discussing matters vital to their welfare.

Higgins also has a Jamesian appreciation of the interplay between character and action—or inaction. As in James, matters of great consequence are sometimes pondered and then left hanging fire in Higgins. But they can also be tackled with speed and élan. Mark Baldwin of *Impostors* plunges immediately into the murder plot hatched to rid him of Sylvia Francis. Some aging sophisticates in *Outlaws*, ordinarily the unlikeliest people to relish the taste of blood, connive at the death of a crime suspect and then gloat when the deed is done. If their ruthlessness inverts the Jamesian paradigm it invokes, it does fit James's view of character. As in works like *Portrait of a Lady*, *Wings of the Dove*, and *Golden Bowl*, the women in *Outlaws* have more guts and nerve than their men. Good intentions in Higgins can bring grief, too, as James showed in *The Turn of the Screw*. Decent, well-meaning people can't help wounding—and getting wounded by—those they love in *Wonderful Years*, half of whose major characters become HIV-positive; in *Defending Billy Ryan*, the dutiful Jerry Kennedy drives away not only Billy but his whole family, as well, by prying information from Billy that, though useful in his defense, shames the old rascal.

33

I

When sex barges into what Peter Lewis called "the tangled network of legal, political, and human relationships" that he saw driving *Rat on Fire*,[3] chaos ensues. Others have noted the disruptive effects of sex in Higgins. Speaking of two journalists in *Impostors*, Nicholas von Hoffman says, "one was caught having sex with an underage girl, and the other murdered his homosexual lover."[4] Also in *Impostors*, Sylvia Francis's empty marriage to a gay man sends her into a love affair she will die of. Another man deserts his wife and kids, one of whom, years later, sees his marriage, the only happy one in the book, ended by a drunken driver. Alcohol continues to work evil. The archetypal Higgins adult male, blue collar or professional, drinks hard and cheats on his wife. In *Victories*, he divorces his decades-long wife to marry a rich blueblood.

Hank and Lillian Briggs should have split long before Hank met Caroline Cook. Nor is theirs Higgins's lone troubled home. Most of the marriages in the canon are unhappy, Higgins becoming a domestic realist in *The Judgment of Deke Hunter* (1976), his fifth novel. In his trademark fashion, Higgins doesn't blame the unraveling of the Hunters' marriage on Deke. To start with, Deke, a state trooper, often works nights. For about a year, he was stationed one hundred miles away from home and only spent weekends with his family. Summers had a greater separating effect. Andrea and the kids stayed at her parents' summer house on the beach, and the weekends Deke joined them were vexing. He had to make the Friday and Sunday evening drives in heavy traffic and, once at the beach, did chores set him by his frail father-in-law, like repairing the family boat and caulking the windows of the cottage.

These chores worsened a problem that Deke had caused. His chiefs sent him across the state to squelch an affaire he was having with a local woman. And now, perhaps in protest, he has found a new girlfriend, strengthening our impression, incidentally, that his creator never decided whether family cohesion is hurt more by booze or adultery. In Deke's case, the two abuses mesh. Deke's amours with Madeleine always follow heavy drinking. What Higgins did, starting with *Judgment*, was to create an emblem for a foundering marriage: [O]ne's car most nights is not in the garage," he said in *Progress of the Seasons*, his 1988 baseball book. Jerry Kennedy insists in his debut, *Kennedy for the Defense*, "I go to my office to make a living, not to make my life. My life is at home" (16). He's wrong. Other people's problems keep pulling him from the nest. They can pull the Higgins hero so far from it that the tie snaps. Earl Beale of *Trust* has a college-age daughter and ex-wife that live at such an emotional distance from him that neither is named on the rare occasions they cross his mind.

The car that's missing from its married owner's garage comes to define original sin for Higgins. The home the owner has made with his wife is where he belongs but—like Nathaniel Hawthorne's Young Goodman Brown—also tends to drift from. And once the drifting starts, it gains force. A trucker who spends nights away from home in *Sandra Nichols* links up with a waitress he marries without divorcing his first wife. When he repents, his first wife only agrees to take him back if he stops trucking and finds work close to home. Needless to say, the troubles of the road could bury the couple. An object lesson they might heed comes in Higgins's short story, "The Habits of the Animals: The Progress of the Seasons," from *The Easiest Thing in the World*. The story hews to a thesis central to George Meredith's *Ordeal of Richard Feverel* and Tolstoy's *War and Peace*, that is, that marriage means being together. A couple must give top priority to their shared life. Partings of any kind hurt a marriage, and, as the ex-GI narrator of Higgins's cautionary tale explains, can also derail it: "Considering Korea and . . . other obligations, I figure we had spent the better part of twenty-two years away from each other, learning things separately that were so different that we ended up never further apart than when we were together" (Easiest, 137).

Partings weaken Henry and Lillian Briggs's marriage in *Victories*. In his days as a big-league pitcher, Hank would spend weeks on the road at a time. His daughter remembers him as "someone who came home on visits" (99). Lillian still frets about spending too much time alone. She deserves a hearing. Hank's current job as a forest warden keeps him away from her the five nights a week he's on patrol, and he also attends the odd banquet to stay in the public eye. What happens next is painful. Often at a loose end, Lillian overeats. Also reflecting Higgins's well-judged sense of consequence, she and the other wives in the canon who feel stranded by their mates protest by blimping up, which lowers the mates' desire to be with them. Lillian reacts to the news that Hank is running for Congress by calling politics another excuse for him to avoid her.

The fat, lonely wife reappears in *Bomber's Law* and *Sandra Nichols*. In *The Rat on Fire* she helps spark a scene called rightly by Higgins "the funniest stuff I've ever written" (CADS 2, 16). The domestic free-for-all begins with the arsonist Leo Proctor hearing from his wife as soon as he comes home at 2:35 a.m., "You smell like a fucking Budweiser brewery." His hot retort, "Well, you *look* like one of them Budweiser horses, you fat old bag,"[5] stokes a hilarious brawl that, besides waking the neighbors, displays Higgins's genius for physical comedy.

There's nothing funny, though, about the legal actions taken against men who have sex with underage girls in *Digger's Game*, *Penance*, *Choice of Enemies*, *Impostors*, *Trust*, and *Bomber's Law*, two of whom, in *Digger* and *Impostors*, are fifteen-year-old Asian-Americans. Erotic imperatives in Higgins continue to raze barriers. A one-night stand with a Hispanic girl during Hank Briggs's ball-playing days ended in the girl's death. *Outlaws* varies the pattern, with different results. In Higgins's 1987 novel, a thrice-married banker of 41 woos and weds a seventeen-year-old only to lose her by carousing with another woman.

Rutting in Higgins often recoils painfully, suggesting, a belief compatible with his Maynooth Jansenism, namely, that all men suffer from sexual guilt. The presence of a (Jay) Quentin in *Impostors* recalls a like-named character in William Faulkner's *The Sound and the Fury* who seduces a lower-class Boston girl. But, unlike his hapless prototype in Faulkner's 1927 novel, the smooth libertine Mark Baldwin buys himself out of the trouble he caused his underage bedmate. Money and social rank often cut across sex in Higgins. Andrew Collier of *Dreamland*, Deke Hunter, Ed Cobb of *Trust* and *Victories*, and Harry Dell'Appa of *Bomber's Law* all marry up. Deke and Harry both romance younger female colleagues. Andrew's father is the hardworking, disciplined son of the founder of a prominent Boston law firm. But the illustrious Cable Wills was also an international con man who, in Andrew, fathered a bastard. Andrew's mother's English bloodlines depict again the indifference of sex to barriers. A gay murder in *Impostors* re-sites the pattern. It also reminds us that unorthodox love ties in Higgins rarely work out. A society matron in *Outlaws* has kept it a secret from her husband that an old family friend fathered the young man they raised as their son. Sexual roguery had already met grief in *Eddie Coyle*, when a banker, showing off to his doxy, a junior colleague, gets shot to death after signaling the police that the bank is being robbed. Overstepping killed Robert Biggers, whose very name, like his assassin's twice calling him a "stupid fuck" (FEC 127) seconds before his death, suggests sins that Higgins, whose early schooling predated the reforms of Vatican II, deems punishable.

Fresh out of high school, Nancy Williams had consensual sex with Biggers, who might have also been her first lover, married or otherwise. Her rutting isn't unusual. She and numerous other women in the canon have sex at will. Higgins's short fiction includes sexually aggressive women in "Intentional Pass," the lead story of *The Sins of the Fathers* (1988), and "The Devil Is Real," from *Easiest Thing*. An oft-wed woman in *Dreamland* who shares their strong sexual itch is called "a goddamned tramp" (28). This term also fits Sandra Nichols and her mother. Bay State women make their sexual needs known. A gangster in *Cogan's Trade* hopes to stay out of jail because, whenever he's inside, his wife finds a lover. Higgins's randy women even develop new needs. The court stenographer Madeleine St. Anne shocks her lover Deke Hunter when she recalls the joy she had servicing three men (" I really wanted them to do it to me" [78]).

Sex keeps causing shocks and dislocations in Higgins, most of which put the family at risk. It's no surprise that Higgins's people often work at the same job for a longer time then they stay married. A judge, for instance, rates his thirty-seven years on the bench in chapter 20 of *A Change of Gravity* (1997) higher than his family life (323). Jobs also outpace love when career advancement beckons. An opening with the New York affiliate of a Boston radio station in *Gravity* ends an announcer's thrice-weekly rut with a Hub politician. In the same book, Diane Fox stays in Boston both to finish her degree and refine her business skills rather than following her economist husband to his new academic post in Chicago. Spousal neglect in the shadow of the workplace worried the creator of Hank and Lillian Briggs for more than twenty years. A New Yorker tells her D.C.-based husband, with whom she dines twice a week in *City on a Hill* (1975), "I like being in New York and working. . . . I also like being married to you, in small doses" (54). The pause, or beat, created by the comma in her second sentence tells all. The husband is wanted, but only occasionally, lest he distract her from what she values most—her job.

The writer Constance Gates of *Impostors* (1986) is another professional woman who worries about balancing sex and work. Connie signs a contract with Mark Baldwin because she has to pay an unruly, ever-mounting MasterCard bill. When asked by a friend if she'd sleep with Baldwin to secure her job, she answers, "He's an attractive man. . . . And it's not like . . . it was a major decision or anything" (I 98). Earlier in the same dinner-table conversation, the man she's talking to warns her that wrongly prepared veal "can be tougher than a biker's jacket" (91). This foreshadowing applies to Connie in ways she'd never have suspected. She'll get her comeuppance when, having already bedded Baldwin, she has sex with another man to advance professionally.

She's away from Boston, playing up to a rural cop with a "round fat face" featuring "teeth heavily tobacco-stained and . . . skin . . . oily enough so that it shone in the orange light" (I 211) of the saloon where she had taken him to lower his resistance. Connie underrated sagging, pouchy Dan Monroe. Not the lout she thought she could charm information out of, Dan teaches her a lesson, namely, that sex is the great democratizer. In his parting shot to her, he says, "We're just the same, Lady Gates. We're identically the same" (226). He and Connie *are* moral equals. They traded sex for information. As in another unlikely sexual pairing in Greene's *Brighton Rock*, there's not a pin to choose between them. If anything, Monroe has bested Connie by playing the dumb provincial slob. But the edge he gained comes at our expense. Like Connie, we patronized Monroe only to leave him feeling dazed and dirty.

It's a poignant moment. Even though she craves connection, every time Connie gets close to a man, she also gets hurt. In a richly ironic passage, the warmth that has been eluding her develops unnoticed and unwatched during a long dialogue with Joe Logan, murderer of the DUI who killed his wife. The sexless conversation, undertaken to help Connie write the article-in-progress for her paymaster Baldwin, covers some 12 hours and swathes chapters 33–40 with only a few breaks. The pair eat, drink, and talk. Having no sexual designs on Joe, Connie responds to him with the full range of her humanity, unconsciously ground-planning a strong erotic bond that has been building on its own. The warmest communion she has with a man in *Impostors* is asexual and, this practitioner of casual sex doesn't recognize it. But will she ever make love to Joe? And has she, through her long chaste interaction with him, already outgrown her boss, Baldwin, who can both destroy her long article about Joe without reading it and, in Sylvia Francis, cause the death of an overly demanding lover? Or should this Jamesian reading give way to the idea that Connie's not sleeping with Joe Logan in the course of book means that she never will (a more truly Jamesian finale?)? This outcome also invites the idea that, in denying Connie the reward of meaningful sex, the Roman Catholic Higgins is punishing her for having made a pastime of sleeping around—if not for mismanaging her funds, a flaw that hurt Flaubert's Emma Bovary more than committing adultery.

The ambiguities permeating *Impostors* justified Richard Somerville, writing as Wormwood Scrubbs, calling Higgins "a brilliant writer."[6] Much of this brilliance inheres in Higgins's ability to describe people under stress (James's "most difficult and dangerous point"?) without inviting us either to take sides or fix blame. As one of Jerry Kennedy's clients in *Defending Billy Ryan* says, patience rates higher than partisanship when dealing with others: "Most guys . . . see everything in black and white, and they forget that . . . most of what is going on is in the gray. That's because there's more of it. More of the gray, I mean" (DBR 67). In *Impostors*, Joe Logan's ability to sink his feelings opens his mind: "Mel Shaw was a good newsman [Joe says of an ex-colleague]. He was hard to get along with. He had something wrong with him. But he could see the importance of things that looked trivial. I didn't like him, boy, but I learned from him" (313).

This same open-mindedness helps Higgins find redeeming traits in the scurviest people. Earl Beale of *Trust* is a scoundrel. The corruption set in early. As a point guard in college, he went to jail for rigging the scores of basketball games. But this "wonder . . . [of] lying and double-crossing" (CADS 2, 10) had the rare hoop skills to tilt the score of a game. And if his ethics as a used-car dealer fall short, they probably compare with those of most of his counterparts. Higgins won't say. But he gave Earl the job of selling cars for a reason. He also matches the job to Earl's life style, deeds, and ways of doing and talking. This diligence improves the book. His practice of wearing his characters' skins rather than passing judgment builds both narrative immediacy and reader involvement. Chapter 16 of *Rat on Fire* discredits the simpleminded responses fostered by hierarchies like the Boston Police Department. Here in the book's midmost chapter, a police lieutenant who has been badgering the rank-and-filers working under him displays his humanity: "My wife's had rheumatoid arthritis for six years now," he says; "She can't get up most days. There are times when she has to use a wheelchair, and I have to feed her. I do the cooking and I do the cleaning and on my way home I do the marketing. [Higgins is again using punctuation, here its absence, thematically, that is., to convey the weight of the speaker's burden by reporting it as a single unbroken unit while also repeating the phrase, "I do," which has taken on a sharply different meaning than it had when the lieutenant spoke it decades earlier at the marriage altar.] She's in pain about every minute. God knows what's been spent on treatments, and I thank God for the medical plan" (RF 114). Anyone who can pluck gratitude from the misery pounding Lt. John Roscommon can be forgiven his excesses. But Higgins doesn't tell us to forgive him any more than he says that Nell Farley's nervous stress disorder in *Wonderful Years* has ruined her digestion and peeled weight from her. More involvingly, he shows the physical and emotional effects of her sickness: "The turtleneck hung loosely on her torso, and the slacks were baggy on her legs. Her feet were planted firmly . . . and her hands were clenched on the arms of he chair opposite her" (122).

Higgins has put himself on a par with his people. The crooks he wrote about his whole career dish out a lot of hard knocks and dirty tricks. But he never acts as if he's slumming by sharing their space. He doesn't even comment on the bullets that drive into Eddie Coyle's brain and end his life. He's not a law-abiding professional describing the atrocities of foul-mouthed crooks to the educated and well-to-do. Rather than patronizing or judging his crooks, he's right there alongside them recording their words and describing their deeds. The apparent ease with which he immerses himself in their brutality builds scenic immediacy and conviction. For instance, what looks like a good-natured schmooze in the last chapter of *Cogan's Trade* ends with two hoods fencing hard for advantage. Narration in Higgins can also ignite drama. The cold deadpan tone of the following description of a seventeen-year-old's introduction to prison life contrasts admirably with subject matter so horrific that flatness suits it better than stylistic heightening: "During his first three weeks in Charleston State Prison, Andy Marr was buggered twenty times, and forced to commit sodomy sixteen times" (JDH 186).

Higgins's sardonic comedy catches the drift of criminal experience. The comedy also resonates. It's up to us to make sense of the grime and the gore. There are no cozy affirmations. As defense attorney Jerry Kennedy says in *Defending Billy Ryan* (1992), the law disrupts peace and wholeness because many of the sharpest legal minds earn fortunes by twisting it: "My job . . . is not to ascertain whether my client did what he was charged with doing, but to make the cops prove it, beyond a reasonable doubt" (172). The client's guilt is secondary. Jerry must put forth his best efforts in what Jean-Paul Sartre might call a "boundary situation." And his lawyering efforts do have an existential backstory, perhaps rooted in writers popular during Higgins's college days, like Sartre and Camus; the dead priest in *Patriot's Game* harks to "The Sisters," the opening story of Joyce's *Dubliners* (a character named Dan Joyce appears in *Trust* [28]). Kennedy has to get close to his clients in order to find information that will help them in trial. But, because most of them are as guilty as hell, he also has to distance himself. How far, though? That the span varies with each client forces Jerry to invent a new set of guidelines every time he defends a crook. This recurring act of self-invention has made him an existential hero.

He keeps improvising new selves without warning. And there's no way of forecasting the realities his ad-libbing will have to adjust to. There's a constant emphasis upon old age in Higgins, which brings puzzlement and incapacity more often than wisdom. Even Higgins's younger people look askance at aging. Getting old worried him from the start. Eddie Coyle died in late autumn (FEC 151) after an uphill fight to stay out of jail, one of his fears of imprisonment having been that he's too old for it (65). Age has started to make Eddie's senior by twenty years, the eponym of *The Agent*, paranoid: "I'm not as young as I used to be, and I sometimes wonder if people aren't trying to take advantage" (56), says sixty-two-year-old Alexander Drouhin, whose control fetish drives him into breaking rules and cheating clients ("He had absolutely no compunction about lying if he thought it'd improve his negotiating position" [A 261], says a colleague). He's suffering from an old man's hurry to expedite work.

Though much younger, a hired gun in *Digger's Game* (1973) works out every day to fight the clinkers of aging. Others are too old to start exercising. Time has already wasted both the senile ex-political boss Otis Ames of *A Choice of Enemies* and the eponym of *Bomber's Law*, a retired police chief so age-racked that none of his ex-colleagues have seen him for years. The closing words of the first chapter of *Dreamland*, "we sat dispirited in the sunlight remaining of the summer" (3), tallies the decline and energy loss that kept the Bomber out of the novel bearing his name. It's natural that time vexes Jerry Kennedy, the person in the canon who most resembles Higgins. Regretful of missed opportunities, the Jerry of *Sandra Nichols*, now living alone, is drinking more than before; his practice has dwindled so much that he has put his secretary on short time; his go-fer Bad-eye Mulvey and his best friend Weldon Cooper are both dead. Age also infuses the short work. "Jack Duggan's Law," from *Easiest Thing*, throngs with images of collapse (e.g. 278). Moody title and all, "Warm for September" begins, "My problem is that I'm getting old, and therefore getting soft" (Easiest 164). With its disquisitions on dying (50) and hearses (58), the book's longest tale, "Slowly Now the Dancer," shows the fading, sagging, buckling effects of age implied by its title; a ninety-year-old dies during the tale's present-tense action.

II

Dishevelment and breakdown can be sidestepped. In addition to the drones, the knee-breakers who work for the gang lords, and the nabobs from Beacon Hill, a host of other characters keeps Higgins's New England fresh and exciting, if not always jolly. Chauffeurs with rap sheets and harried innkeepers looking to cash in on unusually short tourist seasons help flesh out *Trust* and *Wonderful Years*. The novels *Eddie Coyle*, *Patriot's Game*, *End of Day*, and the 1985 short story, from *Sins of the Fathers* (1988), "Balance of the Day," all build heat from the live bullets spurting from the muzzles of contraband guns. Ex-GIs who speak through amplifiers in *Dreamland* and *End* keep danger to the fore. The threat persists. Young urban journalists attract suspicion in *Choice* and *Victories* when they enter New England's backcountry looking for stories. Their names, Rosen and Pokaski, set them off from the locals they have come to interview. These names could also foreshadow the grief these two misfits meet. The car-crash victim Leo Rosen is still languishing at the end of *Choice*, while his counterpart's death in Vietnam, though unrelated to his errand in Vermont, connects to it imaginatively, since Scott Pokaski was sent to Vermont to write a story about a local GI who died in Vietnam, a place whose name has five letters in common with the GI's home state.

Motifs often juice character and theme. Men marry late in *Victories* and *Swan Boats*, Higgins's later phase, starting with the middle novel *Impostors*, featuring the Gothic device of an older man with a younger woman. These bonds are fragile. In the notable funeral director Wallace Weymuss of *End*, Lily Stoat married a senior citizen whose roving eye kept landing him in the divorce court. Lily's second husband, the FBI agent Daren Stoat, who's younger than Weymuss but still a decade Lily's senior, was already resigned to bachelorhood when he met her. Stoat has been rethinking his marriage. A red flag flew up soon after it took place. Rather than following him to Boston, Lily spent the next eight months in D.C. finishing her MBA. Then she used her newly acquired business savvy to put the new house she bought with Stoat in her name; she made the down payment, and he agreed to pay the monthly note and buy the furniture. This deal has recoiled upon Stoat. Lily compounded a blunder in the metals market with the graver one of borrowing against her mortgage; unfriendly changes in real estate investment having deepened her losses in metals. But these reversals leave her unscathed. It's Stoat who's hurt by setbacks that have left him and Lily with less equity in their house than they had when they bought it.

The defeat of an older man by a younger woman explodes more suddenly in *A Change in Gravity*. Lowell Chappell, a bank robber and killer, had spent half of his fifty-seven years behind bars when he met the mentally slow Janet Le Clerc, a welfare client with a prison record of her own living in subsidized housing. The twenty-seven-year-old Janet broke the law when she moved a convicted felon into her digs. Chappell's violent ways with women add to her problems—which burst suddenly. The only way she could stop him from beating her one night was to throw a plugged-in hair dryer into the bathtub he was climbing out of. Nor is she the only backward female in the book. *Gravity* also includes in Donna Hilliard a severely retarded four-year-old who's sent to live permanently in a state home in a desperate, heartbreaking move to save her parents' marriage. Donna casts a shadow. The mentally disabled female, a legacy of Higgins's first marriage (Carlin 23 [M]; Ford, 33, n34), takes the form of sick wives in *Rat on Fire*, *Wonderful Years*, and *Defending Billy Ryan*.

Healthy wives have problems, too. Andrea Hunter explains that her husband Deke has robbed her of a full adult life. She marked time until Deke felt ready to marry her, and, in the decade since, never developed any interests and skills apart from mothering—a real regret now that Deke's career has stalled and some of his wages support an affaire that also cuts into his time at home. The more enlightened, independent wives of Higgins's later work face different worries. Among these is Lenore Emerson of "Slowly Now the Dancer." Lenore teaches a full load at Simmons College while also inching toward a Harvard PhD. Although stressed by this workload, she stays with it; she's the ballerina on a music box that must be wound up lest she slow down and then stop moving. The ballerina, who both supplies the tale's title and appears in its first paragraph, haunts the action. And so does Lenore's husband, Emerson, who picks it up and holds it. But perhaps not for long? Forced to walk on crutches, he moves and stands with difficulty. The ballerina, even when lovingly tended, can only move in circles. It's no wonder that the ambitious, hard-driving careerist Lenore chucks both of them. Highly qualified professional wives and mothers face great pressure in *Choice* and *Bomber's Law* too. The pressure spreads. Joe Corey of *The Mandeville Talent* (1991) may regret quitting his Wall Street law firm to move near Holyoke College, where his wife, a new mother, has a tenure-track assistant professorship. But, during the novel's present-tense action, his house-husbanding frees Jill to move forward professionally while also helping him conduct the investigation that drives the book's plot.

Like Jill Corey, women often have good careers in Higgins's middle and late works. They can also belong to ethnic minorities. Capable Black female judges appear in *Penance* and *Gravity*, at least one of whom, Barrie Foote of *Gravity*, has known domestic woe. She has enjoyed the warmth of the spotlight, too. Her Chicago mother sang so beautifully that Mel Tormé orchestrated her theme song (a fine touch, this, which impresses us all the more because of the tact with which it's offered; Higgins never reminding us that Tormé hailed from Chicago). The glow of the spotlight holds. The judge's second husband is an "internationally known artist" (CG 5), and her hoopster father played in the NBA. As did Junius "Walterboy" Walters of *End of Day*, and he played at a time when pro athletes' salaries were skyrocketing. His counterpart, ex-Minnesota Viking FD Whitman of *The Agent*, came into *his* bonanza through sports agency. Walters, less lucky in his retirement from pro sports, depicts the downside of the changes that have brought Black athletes new freedoms; he deals drugs.

But the same racket that's earning him a fortune has also made him vulnerable. He and his bodyguard are both shot dead during a morning jog, their murderer an older white thug they defied. Here and elsewhere, Higgins's tales of deceit and cunning show crime and the penalties it exacts crossing cultural divides. A novel of upper-echelon conniving, *Swan Boats* traces the overthrow of Yale graduate David Carroll, whose sins as both a husband and a banker merit his fall during an ocean crossing he spends dining grandly and bedding a much younger woman. Street crime is punished more quickly, particularly when it concerns the mob. Perhaps a crook's life is even one of extended punishment. Hoods like Eddie Coyle live not to win but to avoid losing. And losing, short of being killed, means the lockup. Eddie has already done time, and, having been recently caught driving a truckload of stolen goods across state lines, he's heading back. He awaits sentencing. But this little sprat also knows that the law wants bigger fry than he. He'll swap his confederates and chiefs for a recommendation of leniency. In this regard, he has plenty of company. The plotting device of a gang member turning state's evidence has driven crime fiction since the form's inception. Here's Edgar Allan Poe's discussion of it in "The Mystery of Marie Rogët": "Under the circumstances of . . . full pardon to any king's evidence, it is not to be imagined for a moment that some members of a *gang* . . . would not long ago have betrayed his accomplices. . . . He betrays eagerly and early that *he may not be himself betrayed.*"[7]

Plea bargaining thrives, says FBI chief Jack Farrier in *End*. Now that the Mafia's grip on organized crime has loosened, the imperatives of *omerta*, or secrecy, and *rispetatto* count less to a gangster than his fat skin (End 80). But the snitch still can't relax. Neither the police nor the mob care about him as a person. Both are practicing tradecraft, their intransigence a function of long-standing policy. The informer who gets crushed represents collateral damage. The crushing of him rouses little pity or terror anywhere. Having opted to write about the dangers of organized crime, Higgins staked out a place where redemption is rare. The mob's first duty is to protect its turf. Affronts like reneging on a contract or making free with a mobster's near-and-dear will be quashed. The quashing will be dispassionate, surgically efficient, and corporate based, a business transaction rather than the settling of a private grudge. Detective Lieutenant Jim Dowd of *End* knows the usefulness of detached coercion to the mobster: "He [a notorious hoodlum] realized what mattered when you ordered people around was their perception you had the power to hurt them if they didn't [follow orders]" (46). Thugs have icicles in their veins. Survival to them entails violence; kindness and forgiveness are dangerous luxuries.

On the contrary, organized crime rewards brutality and smashes decency. Arthur McKeon, aka McKeach, of *End* learned this lesson while serving as first deputy to crime boss Brian Gallagher. Gallagher's presence on the throne denied McKeach upward mobility. The only way to depose Gallagher was to kill him— which McKeach did by firing thirty rounds at him when he was getting out of his Fleetwood Cadillac (End 43). He had no personal feud with Gallagher. He still thinks kindly of his old chief, whom he always cites affectionately as Brian G. But Brian G stood in his way. As *he* may block the way of someone else? The need to protect himself keeps the mobster's guard up all the time, as Jackie Cogan discovers. The end of *Cogan's Trade* (1974) finds him squared off against another professional crook who, like him, has to keep his heels firmly planted. If such lives run shallow, there's an explanation. Anyone sweating the basics of survival will have no truck with ideas. You can't eat *Das Kapital* or *The Republic*.

But the gangster's survival skills override savage compulsion. If Higgins's hoods didn't curb their savagery, they'd destroy themselves. The collective survival of any group forces its members to work together. Deke Hunter's lecture to his son in chapter 11 of *Judgment* transcends hockey; groups must blend as single organisms. Crooks play by their own rules, which they call good business. They, too, like little leaguers, must bond and practice teamwork. Only by trusting each other can they survive. This strategy, though, flouts a basic disconnect. The climate of *dis*trust crooks function in thwarts solidarity and comradeship. A career in crime requires a flair for deceit and violence. Straight types avoid it. They're wise. As Brian G learned, a crook's safety depends all too often upon what Lenin called the expediency of temporary alliances. Today's ally could become tomorrow's enemy or, worse, assassin.

Higgins uses the adjective, fungible, (RF 66, I 76, DBR 55) and the noun, fungibility (SS 109) to convey the anxiety of his hoods. Fungible means capable of being exchanged. Crime both fosters and speeds the process. It gets worse. The rubbing out of our defining marks to make us better crooks smudges the skills and attitudes that might otherwise help us reform and do regular, honest work. A bookie in *Bomber's Law* "keeps fungible people . . . around" (197) to service his clients. They're like replaceable cogs in a machine that can be discarded once they break or wear out. Operating inside a closed system blocked their freedom to begin with. They exist as parts of a series or continuum rather than individually. Again, they're disposable. And once disposed of, they're forgotten. Fungibility means vanishing inside the void.

A crook's survival instincts are so vital to his trade that they pervade Higgins's fiction from start to finish. McKeach enters Higgins's last novel, *End* (2000), wearing sunglasses, "as always" (28), and wiping his fingerprints from the cardboard sleeve that held the hotdog he just lunched on. A thug in *Eddie Coyle* (1972), Higgins's fictional debut, says, "killing somebody's the surest way in the world to get a goddamned [Higgins always favors this spelling] army after you" (152). Note that the bank robber Arthur Valantrop hasn't condemned murder as a sin. It's just a hindrance to staying out of jail. He's right. An act of violence performed earlier in the book caused two deaths and with them a stepping-up of the investigation of the robbery during which they occurred. Eddie Coyle, who sells sidearms but doesn't fire them, voices the professional gangster's foundation credo soon after walking into the novel: "I get paid for being careful" (5). Careful; not wild or daring; the most successful—and thus most feared—gangsters rate method and order over impulse. Before lashing out, they'll consider other options. Criminals who are more careful than reckless include in their ranks the hit man Short Joe Mossi of *Bomber's Law*, who's called by the cops he keeps foiling "the man that takes no chances" (80–81).

"It seldom happens that a competent hit man is caught in the act. It seldom happens that he is caught after the fact," says Higgins in the nonfictional *Friends of Richard Nixon* (14). In the same book, he also calls "the professional outlaw" "a man of provident humility" (xiv) who plans in advance and, if he needs help with a job, screens his would-be helpers carefully. He stands light years away from the thugs who drove the B-movies made in the era of the silver screen. More of a technician than a desperado, he strives for a quiet efficiency. Also to be shunned is sentiment. The car thief "Cadillac Teddy" Franklin, who appears in all four of the Jerry Kennedy novels, sells the cars he steals on the midnight auto supply within an hour of taking possession. He won't let himself grow fond of a hot car. The efficient crook has to be cold and detached. Like a prizefighter, he works in a dangerous environment and must protect himself at all times.

One self-protective device adopted by all successful crooks consists of hiding one's heart. Jackie Brown wears a deadpan look in the opening sentences of three different chapters of *Eddie Coyle* (he's wearing "no expression on his face" [3, 115, 180]) to hold his style against an interlocutor; stoicism might gain him an edge. This is vital; any transaction in his world is adversarial. Knowing what to say—and what to leave out—helps the crook feign indifference. His tone and body language both say that he's trading the crown jewels for chicken feed, and any sap he's dealing with who rejects his offer is thick. Eagerness needs a mask. McKeach and Nick Cistaro enhance the impression of apathy they've been projecting to two FBI agents over dinner, affecting boredom and inattentiveness when conversational gold starts rolling their way. The weightier the issue, the more casual and nonchalant the demeanor of the hood.

This stock-in-trade ruse makes the hood a master of theatrical illusion. He's not only an actor but also a scriptwriter and a critic who must judge his performance on the fly to steer it in the right direction. He carefully notes tiny details while pretending to ignore them. Higgins has done for the professional crook what Arthur Miller did for the salesman, a spot on whose hat starts an earthquake. But Higgins also invites a question just as serious as that of building and holding an image. What kind of life can this artist-control freak have? Always on his guard, he's no more than an efficient, colorless technician. Morality has drowned in the self-interest that governs his mastery of the details of his job. The tough, unflappable thug is tough and unflappable because he knows that the police could pounce in a heartbeat. To distance himself from them, he spends time on the road, in motor courts, or in hotel bars. Other options? Even when he's not thwarting his pursuers, he's too fixated on his survival to enjoy a healthy family life.

What kind of person, then, becomes an outlaw? Deke Hunter says of a bank robber, "He don't know anything else" (JDH 65). The same can be said about Eddie Coyle and arsonist Leo Proctor of *Rat*, both of whom are planning crimes while awaiting trial for earlier ones they were caught committing. Crime wears men like these two. A predisposition to lawlessness and crime divides them from the square john who works forty hours a week at a steady job. The real-life brothers William and James "Whitey" Bulger grew up in the same Old Harbor slum in south Boston. Like William, who practiced nearly monastic self-denial for years to rise to the presidency of the UMass system, Whitey had academic leanings. An avid reader with a special fondness for history, he enjoyed visiting historic sites, which he may still do, but at tremendous risk. First jailed at age thirteen, he always had a criminal streak. This loan shark, gambler, drug lord, and murderer stands near the top of the FBI's most wanted list, a million-dollar bounty on his head.

The search for him has played havoc with any instinct he might have for steadiness and calm. Like the hoods in Higgins, he can't relax. He wears disguises, uses aliases, and, according to an FBI poster that includes several mug shots, moves between the United States, Canada, Mexico, and Europe. His fictional stand-in, McKeach, is also on the lam during the last several chapters of *End*. He does well to keep moving. Having just murdered two men, he already cooled the trial to himself before the police started looking for him. Perhaps his flight will disrupt his family as much as Whitey Bulger's did his. Not only did brother William lose his UMass presidency and then get his pension slashed for refusing to lead the authorities to Whitey; a third brother, John, or "Jackie," a retired clerk in Boston's Juvenile Court, did time for helping Whitey escape arrest.[8]

Careers in crime hurt the perps' families in other ways. Eddie Coyle wants to avoid another jail stint to spare his children their classmates' jeers. "Beau James" Walker's long incarceration in *Outlaws* tempts his mother to connive at

the murder of the friend whose treachery put her son in stir. The crime committed by Walker and his treacherous friend has sparked a contagion of violence.
Here and elsewhere in Higgins, a felon's freedom is illusory. Earl Beale's sharp-
dealing girlfriend Penny Slate invites Earl to share Thanksgiving dinner with
him; she also couches her offer in terms clear to both of them: "You're not going home. I can't go home either. Us two, we just don't exist" (T 87).

Penny's reneging on the dinner symbolizes for Earl the process by which
crime has been pounding him down. "His life's in a sewer," his brother says of
him (75). His brother is right. Earl pimps for Penny, cheats his customers at the
dealership where he works, and robs his boss. The money he steals, he often
gambles away. His gambling foils him, aggravating his loser's penchant for the
quick fix that has already hamstrung him. Not only does he freelance the Mercedes he was told to take to the scrap yard, he didn't pick up the car when he
was supposed to, either, and in the next chapter, nearly turns up late for another
shady job. The traps he keeps setting for himself have put him in the sewer.

III

Earl's criminal motives aren't deep, primal, or demonic; no demented thriller
hero, he. Neither were they tamed by the time he spent in Fort Leavenworth for
point-shaving. His crookedness stems from within. He, Eddie Coyle, and
McKeach may not like crime any more than the alcoholic likes his glass. Crime
is as basic to these men as their bones and nerves. They never *want* to reform,
regardless of the drawbacks of a criminal existence. Jackie Cogan is told by a
fellow thug, "You can't never do the things you'd like to do. . . . Never. Every
time you do, you get inna shit" (CT 143). At issue here is Cogan's freedom. He
and his kind know that going straight offers more options than the mean streets
and dives of the Hub. The cramped, dangerous lives they have chosen bring the
loss of free will.

So why should we bother reading about them? Higgins doesn't glamorize the
tawdry and the violent. Nor does he show desperate lives tapping into something
grand. What he depicts is his belief in human depravity. Crime, like sex, joins
the gutter to the penthouse, suggesting a unity of thoughts, feelings, and obses-
sions that swathe different races, eras, and locales. This dreadful unity comes
forth in shocking ways. Much of Higgins's genius consists of turning something
ordinary, like the Thanksgiving turkey that goes to waste in *Trust*, and using its
traditional associations with the American family, to say something new and
important.

His main task is trickier still. It's that of bringing to literary life the kinds of
people that fascinate us as images on the movie screen but repel us when they
approach us in buses and lunchrooms. Higgins goes about this task without resorting to lower-depths *verismo*, psychological murk, or slapstick. A sneakily
human realist, he makes us care about his low riders. Eddie and Digger provide

great talk and lively company. It should also be said that both of them flout the standards of the dominant culture. They shake things up. Their crimes have even built a realm skewed from Euro-American ideology. In 1989, Robert Campbell might have had this realm in mind when he credited Higgins with crafting "a world that's realer than real" (Campbell 5X).

This hyperreality can make us wince. Higgins told Brian Doyle in 1991 that his crooks are average people with the same worries and hopes with the rest of us: "People who commit crimes . . . are after money and power, just like every-one else, and they thrash around in the same moral soup the rest of us are in" (25). The names of two big-time felons in *Digger's Game*, Bloom and Green, while perhaps alluding to Higgins's heroes James Joyce and Graham Greene, invoke a prosperity and ease beyond the range of the bottom-feeders in the novel. But, in what's perhaps a reference to Pip's visit to Newgate Prison in *Great Expectations*, these garden images also imply the naturalness of crime; feloniousness remains a possible direction for all of us. And our vulnerability either levels or scrambles moral differences. The murder plot against Eddie Coyle moves forward while he's watching a hockey game attended by 12,000 other people. In *Cogan's Trade*, two hoods plan grand larceny theft while parked in front of a fast-food restaurant that serves hundreds of lunches a day.

A sporting event seedbeds violence again in chapter 24 of *Impostors*. But the plotters aren't washing down hotdogs and beer in the rafters of the Boston Gar-den. They're ensconced in a luxury box at Fenway Park and being served lobster salad by white-jacketed waiters. In a counter-rhythm like that used in the first chapter of Don De Lillo's *Underworld* (1997), the hoots and cheers from the fans in response to what's happening on the field below also refer to the skull-duggery developing in the private box. Ann Janette Johnson reasoned well in the *Detroit Free Press* when she called *Impostors* "a fascinating fictive chess game whose squares are bistros, penthouses, and luxury seaside vacation homes."[9]

Shifting his focus from working-class Boston to the rich suburbs didn't sweeten Higgins's view of humanity. The privileged, socially advantaged pro-fessionals of *Impostors* and *Outlaws* can't claim moral superiority over the hoods peopling Higgins's first three books (parts of which unfold in the suburbs, as well). At times, the hoods seem more down-to-earth. When a crook in *Rat*, another work that takes place in metro Boston, complains about his wild son, his flabby wife, and the high cost of living, he's told, "it's no different for anybody else" (36). Jackie Cogan packs iron. But he also carries a hypodermic syringe to thwart a possible allergic attack on his wife.

In *Trust*, Higgins takes pains to humanize the squalid Earl Beale. Earl lies to his boss to protect a truant co-worker. He helps the co-worker sleep off the ef-fects of the liquor he had been drinking before he staggers into the dealership. With a nod toward Greene's *End of the Affair* (1951), he also leaves his sleeping colleague a container of black coffee to drink when he wakes up (133). Earl owes Roy Fritchie nothing. He has helped him out of goodness rather than self-interest; he gains nothing tangible by tending to Roy's comfort. Higgins has made him likeable and compassionate to certify his humanity. Earl's kindness tempers the muck of his customary cheating. But this tempering action digs still deeper into our shared humanity. By ruling out a knee-jerk moral response to Earl, Higgins has also snagged something dark and elemental in us.

Earl both repels and rivets, Higgins having bared the tension between our facile expectations of what's supposed to be and the chaos of what is. This conjury has blindsided us. But it hasn't knocked us off our bearings. Freud's essay, "The Uncanny," from *On Creativity and the Unconscious* (1925), explains the power of an Earl Beale to both repulse and fixate us. Freud claims, in his influential essay, that something uncanny occurs in civilized people when faced by an abrasive home truth they've been repressing—a primal fear or desire. Earl imparts the shock of the forbidden. It's not only because he, Eddie, and McKeach are thugs. Rather, what shocks is the brazenness of their thuggery. Higgins calls Eddie's murderer Dillon a "psychopath" who "wouldn't consider himself to be a criminal" (Brady 25). Though suspicious and vengeful, he, Jackie Cogan, and Earl suffer no shame. They're less evil than amoral and frighteningly dangerous. A last wall of resistance falls when we watch Earl extending more kindness to his drunken colleague Roy Fritchie than we—who, though not perfect, claim a moral equality, if not superiority, to our friends and neighbors—would muster in a similar situation. The same cheap crook who has dismayed us and even made us laugh has outperformed us, and we feel all the more caught out and exposed because our self-images have been mud-spattered. We've been bested by sleaze in a contest we've already committed ourselves to imaginatively. Earl is one of us.

A combination of shock and veiled shame led the reviewer OCR to call *Eddie Coyle* "unbelievably horrifying yet compulsive reading."[10] Ross Macdonald's own discovery in the novel of something both familiar and forbidding provoked him to call it "the most powerful and frightening crime novel I have read this year" (Just 6K). This same disturbing mirror meeting led Michael Putney to claim that *Eddie Coyle* "reminds you of your own mortality" (21). Putney is talking about Eddie, the book's title character and one of its four fatalities. Not just a cheap crook, Eddie's also a palpable human being, more familiar and even reassuring than monstrous in his efforts, each more desperate than the last, to stay out of jail. These efforts bring to mind Tolstoy's presentation of the villainous Dolokhov in *War and Peace*. Though he's treacherous and vindictive, the great tenderness Dolokhov extends to his mother and hunchbacked sister stops us from damning him outright (the hired gun Short Joe Mossi of *Bomber's Law* brings the same loving care to his retarded brother).

Higgins's linking of crime to banality builds new complexity and depth. A casual reference in *Choice* to Adolf Eichmann (41), whose evil as a war criminal political theorist Hannah Arendt attacked for its banality in *Eichmann in Jerusalem* (1963), invokes Higgins's thematic use of the banal. Banality focuses much of *Bomber's Law* (1993), whose Sgt. Bob Brennan would be recognizable anywhere in Boston. Thirty years on the force have taught this old-school cop to respect the virtues of patience and consistency in crime-stopping. It has also made him *im*patient and resentful of younger, college-educated cops like Harry Dell'Appa, once Brennan's protégé, but now his partner and equal in rank.

There's more to Brennan, though, than his resentment of changes in police routine and personnel the years have brought. He likes to talk about Margaret, his wife of many years. He frets over meeting his Social Security and house payments. He has carpentered a bench in his workshop for his daughter-in-law. Yet that side of him beyond the one that makes homey references to his family, recurring bills, and the prospects of retirement keeps stabbing out. Brennan told Harry's wife Gayle about the love affair with a junior colleague that got Harry exiled to western Massachusetts. His rancor over being displaced on the BPD with younger cops who fight crime with more modern techniques has targeted Harry. Harry personifies the end of his usefulness on the force, an identification that brings out his worst qualities. He also told Gayle that Harry got his much-younger colleague Linda pregnant. This nasty lie, spewed out some two years before the book's present-tense action, rocked Harry and Gayle's marriage so deeply that it's still reeling. It didn't matter to Brennan that Harry had already been punished. Overstepping his authority, "Buffalo Bob," like several other Irish-Americans in the canon who don't know when to stop, fouled the nest of a colleague who made him feel obsolete.

Yet the book's last chapter, in which the rehearsal of Brennan's sins in a detective lieutenant's office leads to his losing his job, brings a shock. Such is Higgins's artistry that it compels our sympathy for this puffy, dead-eyed cop whose "empty holster bobbing on his right hip" (BL 294) symbolizes his impotence. Yes, he's guilty as hell. But as he surrenders his badge and handgun, he's also outnumbered, one of his foes being his immediate superior officer. His "smiling without showing any of his teeth" (274), his calling himself an old man (e.g., 275), and his compulsive chatter all describe him as both out of control and defenseless. But this grizzled old stalwart, who comes apart before our eyes like Herman Wouk's Captain Queeg in *The Caine Mutiny*, knows about defending *others*. He stands for the old guard who both served and protected Bostonians for thirty years, rushing into danger in those days when the BPD was a makeshift paramilitary unit. Though the dynamics differ from those of Wouk's 1951 novel about the U.S. Navy, Brennan's last-chapter dismissal invokes the twinge we felt glimpsing a painfully disoriented Queeg for the last time.

Sgt. Brennan's last job consisted of watching the notorious Joe Mossi. Though Mossi probably murdered eight people on order (BL 140), the police lack the evidence to convict him. They've been waiting in vain for Brennan to catch him incriminating himself. But Brennan hasn't only failed to swoop; he has also watched Mossi and his family for so long that his home has merged with theirs. It's germane that Mossi and Brennan's wife Margaret are the same age (122, 291) and that her first name starts with the same letter as his family name. The bonds in the Mossi and Brennan families also resonate. Brennan's younger brother Douglas (whose bi-syllabic name begins with the same letter as that of Mossi's younger brother Danny) has teamed with Mossi in a scam. Boston is more than a small place in which lives intersect. Its smallness also threatens freedom of choice. Higgins underscores the point by using many repetitions and parallelisms, which, he knows, imply the limits of human opportunities. Brennan tried to flout these limits by either ignoring or burying evidence that would have nailed Mossi. When he says of his quarry, "I feel like I've gotten to know him a little" (14), he's thinking of his shady brother, whom he's trying to protect. But as vulnerable as Douglas is, he's less needy than Mossi's retarded brother. Arresting Mossi would leave Danny unprotected. In no time, he'd die on the street, a fate that vexes the family-minded Brennan.

This, Mossi knows; Iago-like, he has turned Brennan's virtues against him. Shoring up his coldness and cruelty is an eye for human weakness. He'll use whatever advantages he has to protect himself. He'll use them quickly, too. So good is he at avoiding arrest that, by the time Harry Dell'Appa replaces Brennan as his watcher, he has already been researched by Mossi. What Mossi learned will help him pith Harry as he did Brennan. On his first day of work, Harry follows Mossi to a dog track. But the chase reverses quickly, the pursued becoming the pursuer. Mossi plucks the initiative away from Harry by approaching him. Then he adds to his advantage by showing Harry that he knows his weakness. Even before their meeting, he brought his new watcher together with a pretty young waitress who's upset with her married boyfriend, a lug two years Harry's senior. Told in the previous chapter by Gayle, "I understand you look at girls" (158), Harry sees quickly that his private life has become a matter of record; Mossi knows both how to tempt him and hurt him. Harry lost any advantage he thought he had over Mossi even before he met the gunman, who plans to keep it that way.

While responding "idly" to one of Mossi's comments, Harry is also dipping his teabag "repeatedly" in its paper cup. Higgins never says that he's nervous. Instead, he translates Harry's nervousness into a series of tics. Mossi's next words, "Don't talk with your mouth full. . . . It's not polite" (166), refer to a tic that Higgins omitted. The omission was intended. Mossi can exploit the tiniest turn in someone's conduct. He never shows his face in the book again after the dog track scene. He needn't, his lone appearance on the page having already displayed his survival skills. Short Joe Mossi is more than a handful for Harry. Besides having found him an elusive foe, Harry sees that he's also a dangerous one. Such a menace does Mossi pose that, before punishing two pool-playing civil servants for mocking brother Danny, he makes the men beg him to ram their pool cues up their butts. And he does this job with such vim that his two screaming, bleeding victims both need emergency surgery. This frantic episode ("[a]ll kinds of stuff gushing out of their mouths . . . and blood just *spraying* out of their ass" [75]) shows Higgins's anarchic imagination driving a tight plot. Mossi rarely wastes effort. His primitive sense of justice isn't gratuitous, either. Both his victims' willing submission to it before its occurrence and their silence about it afterward ("they didn't complain" [75]) confirm its aptness. Danny can now walk the streets of Boston in peace.

The poise that imbues Higgins's treatment of Mossi's street sense holds when the novels move to Boston's silk stocking district. Like Updike, Higgins was the only child of a schoolteacher who had to moonlight to give his family a decent standard of living. Higgins's penchant for self-disclosure, while less florid than that of D. H. Lawrence, Philip Roth, or James Ellroy, compares with Updike's, too, with its childhood memories of financial constraints. But overcoming these checks carries risks in Higgins. Michael Putney reasons well to say that Higgins's second novel, *The Digger's Game*, was "about how people who commit crimes fit into society" (21); executives in the travel industry have links to both Mafia and Church in this 1973 novel. Organized greed can make the blood sizzle. Robert Campbell discusses Higgins's updating of the Dickensian archetype of the unified society. *Trust* (1989), Campbell says, conveys "the profound outrage Higgins feels about a society that values winning over wisdom, and deceit above honesty . . . and money, money above everything" (5X).

Campbell is on target. The Higgins of both *Outlaws* and *Trust* turns his anger on the white-shoe lawyers, CEOs, and government VIPs who wear designer watches and drive big expensive cars. This anger permeates his whole career. Jerry Kennedy notices the Gucci shoes and Piaget wristwatch of Emerson Teller in chapter 6 of *Kennedy for the Defense*. Then, with a Chandleresque fillip, he sets the conditions under which he'll represent young Emerson, even though he's pinched for cash. Emerson is awaiting trial for having made a sexual pass at a policeman. The still richer Peter Wade of *Sandra Nichols* pays a man to murder a wife he can't get rid of in any other way. Both his and Emerson Teller's wrongdoings suggest that the pioneer sinew that made America great in the nineteenth century has thinned, as in E. A. Robinson, the Eugene O'Neill of *The Hairy Ape* (1920), and Edward Albee's *The American Dream* (1961). This depletion is also noted by Billy Ryan, eponym of Higgins's 1992 novel: "Your aristocratic Yankees—well, in the first place you don't see that many any more. When they run for public office . . . [a]nd when they win, which is not very often, they don't know what to do" (DBR 136).

And the efforts they do undertake usually trip them up, these "white Anglo-Saxon Protestants, raised decently upon the incomes of trust funds amassed by shrewd ancestors" (SS 35). Higgins resents their rentiers' ability to keep feeding their exchequers while some of their luckless neighbors don't have enough cash to live on. But he's also fascinated by them and their trappings, which he can describe with the rapt attention of Bret Easton Ellis. Going heavy on the signals, he opens *Impostors* with a description of Billy Taves, DA for Bristol County, entering the office of a financial mogul he wants to impress:

> The District Attorney was fifty-three years old and had his best suit on, a slubbed silk glen plaid with a muted red stripe he had custom made in . . . the best men's store in New Bedford. His necktie was a Sulka repp stripe that cost him forty dollars in New York, and he was wearing his Johnston and Murphy black-tasseled loafers. (1)

But because Higgins has found that the prizes of the rich lack the luster they had when he glimpsed them as a child, he'll punish their owners by giving them mob ties, bad marriages, and kids who go wrong. The man who doles out these hurts sees himself as a twofold success, in both the law and prose fiction. He calls the Locke Ober Café, the chic Boston restaurant where he was photographed on the dust jackets of his last nine novels, except for *Swan Boats*, "old Boston money, power, connections, stability, security" (Doyle 25). He also knew he could book a table at Locke's at any time. This author of the undergraduate story, "Yesterday, the Gentle Time" (*Stylus* 73 [March 1960]: 34–40), enjoys highly defined civilized pleasures like following the fortunes of old families, their houses, and businesses, and watching Red Sox games from a private box. Although money begets injustice and corruption, it also creates an enviable way of living, and nothing can be done about it. Most of us respond predictably to this rift; a chic Back Bay condo beats a rundown flat in Southie with backed-up toilets.

Higgins's conflictiveness on the privileges of wealth combines features of both Dickens's organic society, where cash and crime walk together in dark, fetid alleys, and Balzac's belief that behind every fortune lies a great crime. But the picture is more knotted. Higgins filtered his reading of these nineteenth-century giants through the lens of his parochial education. While a kind of desperation feeds his craving for the outward show of success, a deeper impulse sparked by his Catholic training scorns these trappings as empty and vain. The scorn has backfired. Higgins often sources the elegance of success in crime. He and Alexander Drouhin, the crooked sports agent in *The Agent*, both delight in travel (Brady 55). His rich Brahmins often drink too much, as did Higgins. Personifying his disquiet with Church writ is Jerry Kennedy, who gets seedier, spend more time alone, avoids going to Mass, and drinks more in each succeeding installment of the quartet of novels he narrates.

Higgins admired John P. Marquand (1893–1960) for his authorial self-restraint (OW 92). But his reprinting ten pages of his fellow Bostonian's *The Late George Apley*, betrays a sentimental streak out of keeping with the quiet irony of Marquand's prose. Marquand wrote about the passing of Boston's Yankee Protestant elite. Transgressing long-held moral scruples, Higgins voices nostalgia for the codes and certainties of these earlier, tradition-based generations. To the end, he remained cowed by old money, old names, and the status conferred by the economic and professional boons that bypassed the home he grew up in. *Dreamland* took him light years from the hard boys and grunge of his first three novels. This "difficult and inaccessible" book, "a favorite of college professors" (Williams 200), looks ironically at the world of old-stock New Englanders. Like *A Year or So with Edgar* (1979), its immediate successor, it tallies at length the rewards conferred by status. It also dwells on the sources of status, chapter 5 of *Dreamland* recovering in minute, loving detail the history of an eminent law firm that formed in 1895 and came to represent powerful Fortune 500 companies from all over the globe. The care Higgins devotes to the Ames family estate in *Choice*, which dates back to 1749, also typifies his fascination with Protestant New England's first families.

But neither here nor anywhere else in the canon will he say as much about his complex attitude to the world of the Apleys—which includes the homage of technical sophistication—as he does in *Dreamland*. A pity because any admirer of Higgins will have to find a used copy of the book; perhaps his most self-referential work, it's also one of the least likely to be reprinted. Andrew Collier, the illegitimate son of the prominent millionaire lawyer Cable Wills, lives in the Wills estate and enjoys all the educational and social blessings of the other children. Compton Wills, the novel's narrator and Cable's *legitimate* son, believes Andrew's father to have died in World War I. He notes, too, that Andrew is a loner. But Andrew also fuels the belief, close to Higgins's heart, that the man who travels fastest also travels alone. Andrew, a topnotch journalist who once interviewed Che Guevera, excels at nearly everything, including, like Patricia Highsmith's sociopathic Tom Ripley, the art of impersonation.

Compton, who both admires and envies him, has little insight into this striver's need to excel. Desperation has prompted Andrew to juice his ambitions with a show of style. The final words of chapter 8 of *Dreamland*, which end the book's first half, "Don't buck the current" (93), apply to him. That he's a crack-shot sailor gives the metaphor added sting. He can't savor his attainments, striking as they are, because he knows that they oppose the tide of his adoptive family's courteous breeding. He can't even enjoy hearing, in this book that opens on a bobbing boat, his father Cable praise his seamanship at Compton's expense. This handy Andy who berths a boat that Compton had nearly disabled must remain an outsider. Like other gifted achievers in American fiction, from Hawthorne's Roger Chillingworth to William Gaddis's Wyatt of *The Recognitions* (1955) and the title figure of Saul Bellow's *Ravelstein* (2000), he lives apart. In college, he gambled recklessly to degrade the prizes that would always elude his grasp. His father Cable noted Andrew's non-belonger's anxiety when he likened him to a Bedouin, or nomad. He has been so busy conning his friends that he doesn't realize the extent to which he has conned himself.

But how much of his own anxiety did the high-flying Higgins write into Andrew? Any cruelty that lodged in the underside of his creativeness surfaces here. Andrew stands for the self-punishing Catholic writer blocked in his quest for WASP gentility. Higgins is the gatecrasher who outperforms the boating set at their own game despite having come to it later in life ("most do not know that there is a Monomoy on Nantucket in addition to the one on the Cape" [D 92]). Andrew "never joined in, never really took part in the happy events [of family life] that included him" (D 21) because he found them painful. The non-belonger bucks the current by rejecting the prize he most covets because, feeling unworthy, he knows he'd waste it. He and Higgins are outsiders by choice. But they play their parts differently. If Andrew is always poised to strike, Higgins cultivates the artist's aloofness celebrated by Joyce in *A Portrait*. His apartness can distance him from the subjects he writes about. By sharpening his perspective on Boston's landed gentry, it can also improve his art. He needn't worry about stifling the flow of blood. His Back Bay swells come to life *because* they have excluded him.

He also knows the sting of exclusion. In *On Writing*, he explains how the "astoundingly underrated" (95) John O'Hara (1905–70) lost his chance for an honorary doctorate by asking for one. He and Higgins have company in the ranks of the snubbed. The artist in Thomas Mann, Joyce, and Patrick White is not just a battlefield of warring impulses but, rather, a misfit whose painful isolation stokes his art. Andrew Collier's skill at imitations has the same source as Higgins's mastery of American speech. Despite having hugged the American dream, these anxious questers have sometimes ventured outside their skin.

The old-money, old-family WASP establishment that Higgins both resents and prizes as a goad figures in most of his work. The banker-father of Bob Wainwright of *Victories* (1990) got rich from timberland snatched from farmer-debtors who, like most of their kind during the Depression, defaulted on their loans. Decades earlier, the founder of the Wainwright dynasty bought his way out of military service like the forebear of *Gatsby*'s narrator, Nick Carraway, who started the family's still thriving hardware business. All the victories in *Victories* are smudged, from Bob Wainwright's fourteen terms in Congress to the ones tasted briefly by the stone loser, Hank Briggs's son, Ted.

Higgins scathes the rich as often as Raymond Chandler, particularly when their wealth connects to the best schools, the right private clubs, and rich established neighborhoods. Yet in *The Long Goodbye* (1953), Chandler's continuing gumshoe Philip Marlowe has joined the white flight to the suburbs, and he values the company of the rich. Higgins shares his fascination. Familiar with the trappings of privilege, he has discovered where old money fish, ski, and eat as well as *what* they eat and wear. He'll make up anecdotes about old money (like the one about a grandee of 101 winters in *Swan*) and even the dead so long as they were gentle born. Sometimes his fascination with Boston's upper crust will take the form of a long description of the origins, charter, and politics of an exclusive private club. His reference to one that stands "three doors east of the intersection of Commonwealth Avenue and Beacon Street" (SWAN 74) prologues a long, meticulous treatise. But Higgins knows that he can't base narrative selection and individual merit on where a character's parents went to school, how much they earn, or where *their* parents came from. To curb his tendencies to linger among the well-born, he'll recover his balance, sometimes self-referentially. Hank Briggs upset his family by marrying a Catholic; a suicide in *A Change of Gravity* is called "a successful man . . . [who] came from modest circumstances" (9).

His reigning in of his pride looks more Protestant than Catholic (Milton, Jonathan Edwards, and Hawthorne come to mind). But it also evokes the two long sermons on the torments of hell given by Father Arnall in Joyce's *A Portrait*, a work whose legacy flickers over the Higgins canon. The gap between Higgins's decent, basically appointed childhood homestead and the posh surroundings of his adult years galvanized a dialectic that harks to Isaiah Berlin's analysis of Tolstoy in *The Hedgehog and the Fox* (1953). Tolstoy, Berlin said famously, is both hedgehog and fox, a pluralist who also possessed a unitary vision. Though driven by the monist's passion for order, he relished life's abundance, as well. Higgins, too, with his oft-used phrase, a "pisshole in the snow" (e.g., A 36), written most likely from his elegant Milton, Massachusetts, study, felt the grip of deep-running contradictions. Did he win money and fame by taking imaginative possession of Boston's underworld? *Eddie Coyle* remains his most successful novel. It might have occurred to this criminal lawyer with an MA in creative writing from Stanford that his tactic of sinking in order to rise resembles that of Satan in Eden. But it's to his vast credit that his inner conflict, rather than immobilizing him, generated that singing tension that sourced his remarkable books.

Notes

1. Michael Putney, "George Higgins: A First Novelist to Reckon With," *National Observer*, 1 April 1972, 21.

2. Edward L. Galligan, "Henry James among the Cops in Boston," *Sewanee Review* CII (Spring 1994): 181.

3. Peter Lewis, "Boston Burning," *TLS*, 15 June 1981, 640.

4. Nicholas von Hoffman, "Making the Newsiest News," *TLS*, 21 February 1986, 183.

5. George V. Higgins, *The Rat on Fire* (New York: Knopf, 1981), 99.

6. Wormwood Scrubbs [i.e., Richard Somerville], "Witty Hiasson Rates Up There with John D," *Des Moines Sunday Register*, 7 February 1988, 4(C).

7. Edgar Allan Poe, "The Mystery of Marie Rogët," *Great Tales and Poems of Edgar Allan Poe* (New York: Pocket, 1975), 192.

8. George V. Higgins, "Whitey and the Rifleman," *The American Lawyer*, July/August 1998, 67–73; Susan Orlean, "Letter from South Boston," *New Yorker*, 26 July 2004, 44–48; See also Howie Carr, *The Bulger Brothers: How They Corrupted and Terrorized Boston for a Quarter Century* (New York: Warner, 2006), esp. 66-67.

9. Anne Janette Johnson, "Prime Elves are Gleaned from Eavesdropping on 'Impostors,'" *Detroit Free Press*, 6 July 1986, 7C.

10. OCR, "Friends of Eddie," *Lewiston* [Maine] *Daily Sun*, 11 March 1972, 4.

Chapter Four

Post-Hardboiled

As Higgins said in both *On Writing* (1990) and the 1978 interview-article on him in the *Dictionary of Literary Biography* (Ruppersburg 237), many writers influenced him. Their influence took different forms. From Dickens comes the impression of a self-regulating urban plenty, the supposedly upright business tycoon (*Dombey and Sons*) or blueblood *(Hard Times, Our Mutual Friend)* whose fortune has roots in crime, and the already mentioned motif, taken from the Jarndyce vs. Jarndyce case in *Bleak House*, of the legal action that leaves its litigants dazed and empty-handed. The madness gripping Bill Sykes as he flees the London police in *Oliver Twist* and the murder puzzle driving Dickens's unfinished *Edwin Drood* put forth a vision of terror that influenced the American thriller more than it did either the English mainstream fiction of F. R. Leavis's Great Tradition or the Golden Age mysteries of Dorothy L. Sayers, Margery Allingham, and Agatha Christie. Whose work Higgins knows; his reference to "little gray cells" in *Penance* (209) and one character's assessment of another in *Kennedy for the Defense*, "He's so smart, he doesn't act smart, and that is really smart" (231), both come straight from Christie's dapper little Belgian sleuth, Hercule Poirot. Poe, whose distant, enigmatic C. Auguste Dupin gave rise to Poirot, colored Higgins's work from its outset. As in "The Purloined Letter," two federal agents in *Eddie Coyle* try to enter the mental flow of a gangster (viz., Jackie Brown) in order to forecast his moves in order to catch him in a criminal act. The motif of a criminal suspect ratting on his confederates in exchange for leniency from the bench, also prominent in *Eddie Coyle*, led Dupin to the murderer of the title figure in "The Mystery of Marie Rogët."

Two more American writers Higgins admires are Ernest Hemingway and John O'Hara, whom he prefers to Scott Fitzgerald (OW 95). Like Higgins, O'Hara wrote a ton, sometimes about car dealers. Higgins's crediting him with having "the eye of a recording angel," while aping Ross Macdonald's claim that Raymond Chandler wrote "like a slumming angel,"[1] presumes a ruthless honesty that Higgins prized himself (OW 109–10). O'Hara might have caught Higgins's eye because the younger writer saw so much of himself in him. Only children from the east coast who grew up humbly, both men earned blue-chip academic degrees (the Pennsylvanian O'Hara matriculated at Yale). Lovers of classic cars, both Irish-American Catholics also drank too much, a failing that might have wrenched their marriages. But first and foremost a fiction writer, Higgins devotes more pages to O'Hara (93–120) than he did to any other writer he discusses in *On Writing* because O'Hara excelled at short fiction; of his 374 published tales, Higgins puts "at least three dozen . . . in the first rank" (OW 97). Higgins, regrettably, never had much success with the genre. His first shortstory collection, *The Sins of the Fathers* (1988), was published only in the UK. *The Easiest Thing in the World*, his second, did find an American publisher but not until 2004, five years after his death, and it made little splash. Whether or not Higgins foresaw this humble reception, it promotes the argument that, like many other writers, he prized most in O'Hara a gift he himself lacked.

Preferring from the start writers who, like O'Hara, valued economy and sinew over the copious and the profuse, Higgins recalls being "thrilled" when he read Ernest Hemingway's "Big Two-Hearted River" at age eleven (CADS 1, 20). Hemingway's tight, accurate prose stayed close to Higgins's heart. The shotgun blasts biting into the "maxillary, zygomatic, nasal, temporal, and frontal lobes" of a murder victim in *The Mandeville Talent* (1991) refer to the cold accuracy of Hemingway's description of a shooting death in "The Short Happy Life of Francis Macomber" (1936). A 1963 Higgins story, "All Day Was All There Was," which mentions "Big Two-Hearted River," starts with a nine-year-old on a fishing expedition with his uncle. Another story published the same year, "Something Dirty You Could Keep," unfolds in wartime Italy,[2] as did Hemingway's *A Farewell to Arms* (1929), the first chapter of which Higgins reprints as a model of excellence in *On Writing* (28–30).

Interestingly, both of these fledgling tales eschew dialogue, a shock to any tracer of the growth and development of Higgins's art. "My characters tell the bulk of their stories" (11), he said in the unpublished "Dances with Muses." But some of his best effects bypass dialogue, Higgins facing the reader directly. These effects could also reflect his reading. If the title of "Something Dirty You Could Keep" evokes the second story of Joyce's *Dubliners*, "An Encounter," it might also be apt to note the repetitions, parallels, and mirror images that stoked Joyce's cosmic comedy in Higgins's later work. Behind this Joycean brew in Higgins sits the town of Proctor, near Salem. The handyman who uses his training and skill to commit arson in *Rat on Fire* (1981) is called Leo Proctor. Three years after the publication of *Rat*, in *A Choice of Enemies*, a man dreams he's in church in Proctor (128), where some of the novel will unfurl. The oft-used reference could easily come from Arthur Miller's *The Crucible*, which both takes place in Salem and includes a family named Proctor. Finally, Proctor, Massachusetts, has both a Higgins Middle School and a Higgins Field. But a Higgins novel, like Miller's great 1953 play, also reflects its own time. A thug in *Deke Hunter* (1976) who gets caught "stealing a sizable coin collection" (182) calls to mind David Mamet's *American Buffalo*, which, besides premiering in 1975, also has as its main action a plot to steal some coins.

The literary borrowings of this busy author of hundreds of articles, columns, and reviews as well as thirty books cover a broad range. Graham Greene, whom he cited in a 1975 interview, provides an influence (Brady 52), most notably his celebrated Judas complex. As in Greene, love runs aground of betrayal in Higgins. The short fiction (where, less sure of himself, Higgins is more prone to borrow from others) supplies some good examples. Harking to Greene's *Fallen Idol* or "Basement Room" (1949), the 1998 story, "A Martini for Father McBride," features a boy who, having innocently incriminated a family servant he loves, morphs into the self-blamer that drives many of Greene's books like *The Ministry of Fear* (1943), *The Heart of the Matter* (1948), *The Third Man* (1950), and *The Captain and the Enemy* (1988). In Higgins's "An Interview with Diane Fox," the self-blamer is an inconstant wife. But Higgins's theology veers from Greene's, holding little truck with miracles, the raising of the dead, and the puzzling nature of God's grace, even though he uses some of Greene's favorite symbols, namely, the cracked bell in *Billy Ryan* (96), which evokes an unhappy childhood in *England Made Me* (1935), and "the green baize surface" of a billiard table in *Trust* (169), suggesting the frontiers occupied by outcasts and outlaws in much of Greene.

The cradle Catholic Higgins finds life less of a spiritual struggle than the convert Greene, with his acquired sense of horror and moral urgency. Yes, the youth of *Eddie Coyle*'s Jackie Brown, like that of Greene's Pinkie Brown in *Brighton Rock* (1938), intensifies his evil; the malevolence of both youngsters emit a harsh purity hostile to the concessions of growing up and becoming socialized. But Jackie's malevolence rouses less fear than Pinkie's (and requires less need for a miracle) because it ignores sexual passion and Church law. If Jackie Brown had a sex life, he'd manage it with the same insouciance displayed by Higgins's other bed hoppers (except for the ones who discover, in *Wonderful Years*, that they've become HIV positive). The soul-wrenching love affair that Greene had with Catherine Walson, the married mother of five, provoked in *The End of the Affair* a spiritual drama without counterpart in Higgins, whose Catholic priests dwell more on their creature comforts than on the mystery of God.

Sometimes a reference to another writer will stand as a tribute rather than suggest a line of influence. *Billy Ryan* includes a lawyer named Andy Keats. Some "swallows rustling" in a barn above the head of Hank Briggs in *Victories* (20) and some "barn swallows" in "Slowly Now the Dancer" (*Easiest* 82), besides voicing Higgins's admiration for Scott Fitzgerald's favorite writer, also show his awareness of the importance of tactile values in a literary work. But it's Keats's "Isabella, or The Pot of Basil," not "Autumn," that includes a murder. The family context of the murder invokes one of the finest crime novelists of the last century, Ross Macdonald, in whose work corpses are planted, not buried. As in James Ellroy's *L.A. Confidential* (1990) and most of Ross Macdonald's books, murder cases that were either unsolved or improperly solved in both Higgins's *Impostors* and *The Mandeville Talent* reopen twenty years later. Admittedly, the two hundred years between Keats's birth and Higgins's death have thinned the line of literary descent joining the two writers who also lived an ocean apart. But anyone who wants to slice or bury the line should note that Ross Macdonald, using his real name, Kenneth Millar, wrote his PhD dissertation on Keats's older contemporary and fellow Romantic poet, Samuel Taylor Coleridge.[3]

I

Which other writers impressed Higgins? There's evidence to back Elmore Leonard's claim that Higgins didn't "come out of the Hammett-Chandler school of crime writing" (Easiest, vii). Whereas none of Higgins's novels begin as a missing person's case, Hammett, Chandler, and their disciple Ross Macdonald used this motif to launch every novel they wrote. Nor does Higgins use a continuing detective-narrator like Hammett's Continental Op, Chandler's Philip Marlowe, or Ross Macdonald's Lew Archer. The reason: crime-stopping means less in Higgins than does the act of crime and its litigation. Higgins's denial that he wrote crime fiction (Williams 205) gauges the distance between *his* art and *Black Mask* aesthetics. His belief in man's fundamental dishonesty ("most people are dishonest") led him to invent characters "a number of whom have a tendency to break the law" (Bannon 26). This Augustinian projection of a fallen humanity makes crime the lifeline between people, putting his fiction in a dark subcategory of its own. Look at his ontology. His statement, "I don't think there's any such thing as "criminal"" (Bannon 26), posits a depravity that calls forth the moral chaos described by Jim Thompson.

But the invocation only extends so far. If Higgins owes little or nothing to Hammett and Chandler, as Elmore Leonard says, he remained aware of these writers his whole career. His fine December 1972 *Esquire* piece, "The Private Eye as Illegal Hero," sharp-focuses these two hardboiled writers along with Mickey Spillane and Ian Fleming.[4] Higgins's ongoing awareness of Hammett always came forth as a tribute. "The Devil Is Real," which debuted in the March 1986 issue of *Playboy*, includes a James F. Teal, who never appears.[5] The eponym of Hammett's "Who Killed Bob Teal," from *True Detective Stories*, November 1924, like that of Hammett's *Thin Man* (1934), died before the story opens. *Sins of the Fathers* also includes in "John Tully's Jaguar" (117–34), a story whose title, an encapsulated entity, fits the pattern of Hammett's "The Scorched Face," "Fly Paper," and "Dead Yellow Women." "Intentional Pass," also from *Sins of the Fathers* (41–51), blends Fitzgerald's light with that of Hammett. Building from a premise set forth in Fitzgerald's 1926 story, "The Rich Boy," that is, most lovers intuit the moment when they must cement their bond or lose it, a lawyer uses innuendo and analogy to distance a woman who wants to connect with him. Sam Spade used the same verbal strategy with Brigid O'Shaughnessy in chapter 7 of *The Maltese Falcon* when he told her about Charles Flitcraft (the Flitcraft device will recur in chapter 16 of *Billy Ryan* and chapter 19 of *Sandra Nichols*, but with less success).

Some of Higgins's tributes to Hammett will take the form of a phrase. Craig Emerson's words in "Slowly Now the Dancer" (Easiest 93), "there was merry hell to pay," lift a metaphor from the last sentence of Hammett's *Red Harvest* (1929). A man who praises a woman in *Impostors* uses the same words, "You're very good" (52), that a charmed Sam Spade did with Brigid O'Shaughnessy.[6] This coincidence could be shrugged off had Higgins not mentioned Spade in *Choice of Enemies* (292) six chapters after introducing a cop named Danny Shaughnessy (183). Also from *Falcon*, the device of reporting only one side of a conversation, for instance, Spade's response in chapter 2 to the news of his partner Miles Archer's murder (11), runs through all of Higgins's work (e.g., FEC 171-2, CE 29, I 151). Even Higgins's nonfiction echoes *Falcon*. Spade's remark to Wilmer Cook, "the cheaper the crook, the gaudier the pattern" (120), returns in *The Friends of Richard Nixon* as "The more devious the crook, the more sanctimonious the patter" (238). One flaw, hardly worth noting, pits the surface of Higgins's career-long tribute to Hammett—his misuse of the word, gunsel (e.g., MT 126, BL 189, End 43). When Spade calls Wilmer Cook a gunsel (110), he's imputing feminine traits to him; Higgins uses the term as a synonym for gangster, which it sounds like.

But is Higgins's elaborate Chandleresque conceit, "The Coach's lips hung from his face like strips of wallpaper in the hands of a man with a ladder,"[7] a tribute gone wrong? No; the conceit distorts only slightly Chandler's verbal wit, such as that found in chapter 2 of *The Big Sleep* (1939), which describes Marlowe's legendary introduction to a dying General Guy Sternwood, whose scalp discloses a "few locks of dry white hair clung . . . like flowers fighting for life on a bare rock."[8] The meeting of Philip Marlowe and General Guy Sternwood impressed Higgins. "The Balance of the Day," from *Sins*, includes the phrase, "a few white hairs trailing over the mottled scalp" (63–64). Written early in Higgins's career, namely, 1969, this conceit follows the basic rule of caricature— exaggerate your subject's most notable trait. Higgins's high regard for *Big Sleep* resurfaces often. As in Chandler's debut novel, smutty photos move the plot of *Sandra Nichols* (1996). The narrator of *Edgar* (1979), Peter Quinn, voices a professional manifesto redolent of that of Marlowe in chapter 30 of *Big Sleep*. Here is Marlowe talking to the General: "*You* don't know what I have to go through . . . to do your job for you. . . . I do my best to protect you and I may break a few rules, but I break them in your favor. The client comes first, unless he's crooked. Even then all I do is hand the job back to him and keep my mouth shut" (212–213). Now, Higgins's version: "I'm your lawyer. I tell you what I think you ought to do. And if it's not liable to get me disbarred, I obey your instructions. . . . Unless doing so would make me look like a goddamned fool, in which event I tell you to go plague another lawyer" (Edgar 125).

Away from *Big Sleep*, both the words spoken by a beer drinker in *Victories*, "Ahhh . . . first of the goddamned [that spelling again] day. Always tastes the best" (30), and a bank teller's pronouncements in *Mandeville Talent*, "I've always liked that first one of the day" (16), reprise Terry Lennox's indelible words to Marlowe in chapter 4 of *The Long Goodbye* (1953): "I like bars after they open for the evening. When the air inside is still cool and clean. . . . I like to watch the man mix the first one of the evening. . . . I like to taste it slowly. The first quiet drink of the evening in a quiet bar—that's wonderful."[9] Characters named Marlowe and Malory, Chandler's original name for Marlowe, in "Slowly Now the Dancer" (Easiest, 69, 82) argue that Higgins's awareness of Chandler persisted throughout his career. Apropos of nothing, *Trust* uses the words, "the high window" (162), which also stand as the title of Chandler's 1942 novel. Why Chandler came to his mind more often than Hammett, whom he also admired, may hinge on the question of style. Besides having grown up in England, Chandler was the more conscious stylist. His highly developed prose may have also captured the mood of urban anxiety central to much of Higgins.

An influence more subtle yet more substantive than these two detective writers is Higgins's older contemporary, William Gaddis (1922–98). That both east-coast writers relied heavily on dialogue suggests that the influence might have been mutual. The phrase, "a frolic of his own," appears in *Richard Nixon* (152), some nineteen years before the publication of Gaddis's novel of the same name. It returns in *Outlaws* as "frolics of their own" (343), and Higgins's discussion of its meaning in *Swan Boats* (70) closely paraphrases Gaddis's (1994; 298). The lawyer Higgins might have vetted Gaddis's 1994 novel about the law. In *Sandra Nichols*, the flow of a lawman's statement, "The only places where the case *always* ends with the killer getting caught are the ones you see on TV" (55), recalls the opening words of *Frolic*, spoken by a lawyer, "Justice?—You get justice in the next world, in this one you have the law" (11).

This echo resonates. Gaddis outstripped Higgins as a novelist, and Higgins knew it. His tribute to this knowledge takes different forms. The 1986 story, from *Sins*, "The Devil Is Real," treats counterfeiting, a major trope in Gaddis's first novel, *The Recognitions* (1955). It would be sophomoric to note the sameness between the initials of Connie Gates of *Impostors* (1986) and those of the title of Gaddis's *Carpenter's Gothic* had Higgins's next book, the 1987 *Outlaws*, not included a character who, like someone in Gaddis's 1985 novel, lives in an ashram. The salutes to his mentor pile up. *Wonderful Years*, coming out in 1988 and thus belonging to the same creative phase as *Impostors* and *Outlaws*, contains the sentence, "War is the extension of diplomacy by other means" (173), a close replica of words spoken in *Carpenter's Gothic*.[10] The phrase, "some of her got blown back into our faces—ashes—sprinkling and scattering" (41), from *Bomber's Law*, completes the cycle; similar phrasing appears on the first page of Gaddis's second novel, *JR* (1975).

One of Gaddis's ideas might show up in Higgins as well as a literary conceit. The weightiest of these has to be entropy. This second law of thermodynamics tallies both the disorder and the energy loss within a system. Gaddis referenced it in *JR* when he called order "the thin perilous condition we try to impose on the basic reality of chaos" (20). Disorder rules. Higgins addressed the problem of living amid breakdown and upheaval in *Victories* (1990), where he calls entropy "the point at which a system overheats and disintegrates" (294). *Victories* is also where a science teacher defines Heisenberg's Principle ("When you measure a system, you disrupt it") and then calls his small New England town "a very closed community" (258).

Speeding the entropic drift that downgrades solid matter to sludge in Higgins is crime; breaking the law thwarts our efforts to fight chaos. Though hired to protect the flora and fauna in his district of Vermont, Hank Briggs watches death have its way. The novel's first chapter shows this forest warden taking no action against a poacher who jacklit and then shot a deer. The shooter is that familiar legacy from Joyce's "The Sisters," a guilty priest. Whom Hank lets slide; his disloyalties to his Catholic wife Lillian stay his hand against Father Morrissette, whose animal-like nickname, Bunny, also rouses Hank's protective instincts. The novel's Christian framework holds. Later in the book, a teenager dies when a bullet intended for a snake rebounds off a rock and hits him. The drift toward dissolution in *Victories* is so strong that no heat is needed to speed its destructive effects. (Entropy is often called the "heat-death.") In fact, the novel refers frequently to Vermont's long, hard spells of cold weather. Hank, more than five years from his glory days as a major leaguer, has put on weight, though not as much as Lillian. Their balding spendthrift son was a poor student who can't hold a job as an adult of twenty-four.

Collapse and waste are handled differently in *Outlaws*. In chapter 38 of Higgins's 1987 novel, a detective refers to a colleague as "an asshole," calling his interlocutor "an anus" as well, a condition that leaves him "trying to shine shit" (287–88). References earlier in the book included on a single page "a pissing contest," a "goddamned pile of turds," and "three pounds of shit in a two-pound bag" (16). Higgins has traced the curve of entropic decay. Preceding the undifferentiated blobs created by entropy is the loss of defining marks. *Outlaws* opens with a bank robbery and then jump-cuts to a discussion of "an internationally known orchestra" (3) that's playing Mozart more than a continent away in Alaska. These far-flung events will fuse in an entropic flow that ends in death. Fungibility (e.g. 176, DBR 55) enters here, too, as identities blur into each other. The blur, or stain, has spread. Rather than enjoying free-standing selfhood, Cpl. Molly Dennis, who appears in a rural Massachusetts DA's office (68, 287), exists in series with the doorman of a London hotel she has never met named Dennis (299).

Symptoms of decline tighten their grip. A person in Higgins's next novel is called "frail . . . and . . . old beyond her years" (WY 236). (Another guest in the inn where she has gone to recuperate has AIDS, which, he believes, will kill him.) Rather than recuperating, Nell Farley dies. The words of one of the skiers who discovers her corpse on a slope, at the end of the book's next-to-last chapter, "It's all downhill from here" (237), prove prophetic as well as topographically apt. The transfer of Nell's corpse down to the inn where she was staying gives way to a funeral and still another death. The death drift has gained force. Implied is that the AIDS victim will die and the inn where he's staying, fold. Equally possible is a surge in the disorganization and collapse that attend AIDS, which has already infected about half of the book's characters.

Higgins had portrayed some of the dangers of self-enclosed systems in *Outlaws*, which extends its perimeters to blazing Morocco (275) and whose openness to heat-death also moves the book's plot. Entropy does its work elsewhere, too. An accomplished elder who calls history "a pattern of repetition" has also foretold the loss of energy, an effect of entropy. Repetition in Dante and Nietzsche denote entrapment, even hopeless enslavement. Freud equates it with the death wish. But Higgins is a literary artist, not a cultural philosopher. The elder continues: "Every generation has strived to sacrifice its parents. . . . If we are, in fact, all outlaws, it has been of necessity" (O 337).

Higgins's treatment of intergenerational tragedy belies this determinism. With a Brechtian fillip, he'll stand it on its head. A matron in *Outlaws* who believes that her grown daughter Christina needs stability (357) has built her life around adultery and violence, including, most recently, murder. A musician, Christina inclines to harmony. But, like most of the book's other characters, she finds it elusive. The book's last chapter shows her lover wrestling with the details of his divorce. Meanwhile, her brother James is serving a long prison term as a result of having been betrayed. His betrayer? Sam Tibbetts is both Christina's lover and the victim of the murder plot hatched by her and James's mother.

Bizarre and convoluted? If *Outlaws* looks like a demented well-made play or screwball comedy gone haywire, the resemblance is intended. But the book isn't overplotted. The deforming, disfiguring effects of entropy always subside into a hodgepodge. That the hodgepodge swathes Alaska, greater Boston, and Morocco extends the decree of former Speaker of the House of Representatives, Thomas P. "Tip" O'Neill, "All politics are local." A. J. Johnson hit the mark when she said that the Higgins of *Impostors* "has been around the block a few times and knows his turf—right down to which rugs hide the worst dust" (7C). Her argument is worthier than she knows. Dirt is so pervasive and so self-generating in Higgins that a wilderness of rugs couldn't hide it.

It's endemic in *End of Day*, where a profitable drug ring runs afoul of greed and misjudgment. The ring's boss orders more product. Because his pronouncements are law, his stooges obey him. (When asked, "who the fuck is Guido?" the title figure of *Edgar* answers, "Making Guido mad is not a good idea. . . . Whatever Guido wants, Guido gets" [219–20]). He has overlooked the wisdom of Occam's razor. Expanding the ring also weakens it, subjecting it to the ravages of entropy. The small-scale but smooth-running drug racket that oversteps its bounds courts danger; a pharmacist who routinely fills a monthly order for a forged prescription will balk if he sees the order once a week. Trouble in Higgins often stems from not knowing when to stop.

Politics can't supply the brake. *Choice* and *Wonderful Years* both show building contractors paying politicians so much in kickbacks and bribes that their profits shrink beyond the point of acceptability. Compromise is no answer. Meeting politicians' demands will force contractors to scrimp on labor and materials, a step that invites shoddy work. Power corrupts differently in *Outlaws*. The student rebels who rob banks to fund humanitarian causes adopt the ugliest policies of the establishment they want to overthrow. Impatient with the give-and-take of democratic process, the head of the Bolivian Contingent uses strong-arm tactics: "We're gonna have discipline in this group . . . because . . . absolute discipline's the only way we can survive" (247). Yet bullyboy Sam Tibbetts is the only member of the Contingent who avoids jail, his freedom coming, ironically, from the Brookline family money and connections that hallmarked the alleged fascist domination he had set out to crush—using fascist methods. What's left is moral murk, the logical upshot of his malcontent's hidden agenda of supporting a war of all against all.

II

Higgins heeds this chaos. As has been seen, hard work, usually done in groups, can tame it. His art reflects this effort. He'll write about corporate or political greed without pitting a hero against his oppressive or anarchic state. This effort shows him bucking precedent. In both the police procedural and the American private-eye novel, society itself is the culprit. The crimes committed in the work of Chandler, Ed McBain, and James Ellroy bespeak corruption; a missing-person's case can foretell wrongdoing in a corporate giant like today's Nike, Citigroup, ExxonMobil, or MTV. Like major artists of all stripes, Higgins, by siting trouble elsewhere, defies trends, traditions, and even labels. The small-time racketeers from his early work recall the ones found in pulp magazines like *Dime Mystery Magazine* and *Black Mask* that television shut down in the late 1940s and 1950s. Yet both Higgins's narrative stance and carefully wrought prose couldn't stand further from the pulps that left their stamp on him. Absent too from the canon is the stoicism and reserve of the hardboiled dick of yore, like Carroll John Daly's Race Williams.

Time rolls backwards in traditional detective stories with their sleuthhounds identifying spoors and following tracks in order to connect crimes to their origins. In the English country house mystery, evil will be stamped out; the murderer, if not caught and punished, will die. The American hardboiled mystery, unfolding in a corrupt society of paid-off judges and cops, shows the criminal strolling out of court with a suspended sentence. The big-time racketeer Eddie Mars of Chandler's *Big Sleep*, with friends in high places in City Hall, never even stands trial. Looking in a different direction, Higgins specializes in the daily routine of criminals and the criminal acts they perform rather than crime's detection. Except for the late *Mandeville Talent* and *Agent*, the novels avoid forensics in the form of medical examiners' reports or a crime lab's analysis of blood samples under powerful microscopes.

Neither do they seek to shock, moralize, or build suspense. Even before taking a case, Jerry Kennedy presumes his client's guilt; his job is to stop the DA from proving it. No servant of justice, he. Except for the work he does to secure the financial future of Sandra Nichols's orphans, he cares little more about morality than Jim Mandeville's hired killer, that is, the talent, in *The Mandeville Talent*. When reminded that he used to be Mandeville's friend, the talent replies, "This has nothing to do with that. . . . I do what the boss says" (8). Then he shoots Mandeville. Whys and wherefores he stifles, as he does any emotional investment he has in the contract. He's paid to do a job. And that job, like Jerry Kennedy's, lacks Freudian roots. Higgins avoids the parents-mess-you-up novel. In fact, works like *Wonderful Years*, *Victories*, and *Billy Ryan* show parents paying for their kids' missteps.

Higgins executes this reversal without resorting to the lurid tabloid effects of James Ellroy. He also shuns Jim Thompson's homicidal maniacs and turbocharged grotesques; his people aren't racked by dark lusts. Though pessimistic, this crypto-Jansenist provides no overarching vision of damnation. But the opposite holds true, as well. His books are as free from the cult of atonality and anomie as they are of creeping atavism. Higgins picked up themes from American gangster movies, the pulps, and the clients he represented and then, thanks to his whipcord prose, lyricized them.

He also probed their subtext. As in most tribal groups, the organized crooks and businessmen, cops and pols, he writes about live by rules, even unwritten ones. Only when an honored constraint is flouted will the capos' cavemen act— but more out of a sense of embattled integrity and honor than raw anger. Such moments reach us in a voice that warns the reader that his/her comfort will be ignored. The rough stuff in Higgins flouts the courteous reader-writer collaboration. Instead of coddling his knowing readers, Higgins's best-known books have as their staple an urban vernacular. He has challenged the popular literary tradition he grew up in. If local realities matter, they take on more color and bite when voiced in the local idiom. This is the same idiom that helps neighbors know and trust each other. Speech in Higgins expresses social bonding and belonging.

The third-person narrating voice, a corollary of both Higgins's successful law practice and narrative tradition, could drift into a paternalism that must be quashed if it's to keep faith with a Digger Doherty or a McKeach. First, it clashes with the milieu Digger and McKeach inhabit and, in less capable hands, might mock or sensationalize that milieu. Higgins solves the problem by moving his narratives with dialogue. Getting inside his thugs' psyches lets him convey the pressure the thugs feel every day. His statement about point of view in fiction, "generally I use the omniscient narrator" (CADS 1, 32), has to be qualified. Though omniscience enables an author to both summarize and provide interscenic commentary helpful to the reader, Higgins avails himself of these benefits while shunning those other standbys of the technique—interpreting the story and drawing morals from it. Such intrusions both harangue readers and distract them from the people.

In Higgins's case, that would have been a pity. His work as a prosecutor, having taught him not to expect too much from people, created many outlets for narrative excitement we'd not have wanted to miss out on. But there's more. In 1975, he said that *all* the defendants he helped convict deserved jail time (Brady 27). Yet he also knew that intruding this sour view of humanity into his fiction would block the broader moral effects good fiction has always provided. Thus events in his work usually reach us from the mouths of the participants. His omniscience fades into his characters' words. Rather than scolding or trying to reform the characters, he abandons them to the starkness, even the brutality, of their speech. Many of the descriptions in the early work rise from dialogue, memories, and impressions that surface while the people are telling their stories. As in Henry James, Joseph Conrad and Ford Madox Ford, objective reality means less to Higgins than someone's experience of it.

Higgins's success with this point-of-view technique rests on his genius for climbing into the heads of louts and thugs. When crafted properly, the technique allows him to be sneakily profound without buckling to banality. His ability to throw fresh, revealing, nonjudgmental light on characters who are childish, violent, and racist makes us swear we knew these crooks, despite never having met them. Higgins's strategy of moving the edges to the middle also creates scenes too stark in their recognitions for readers of popular mainstream fiction. Cleaving to Joyce's account of the growth of literary art from the lyrical to the epical to the dramatic in chapter 5 of *A Portrait*, Higgins at the top of his game dramatizes the events of his novels; his people take over the action. Grey Gowrie might have been thinking about Higgins's gift for bringing his books so close to life when he called him a "great classical novelist."

Is Gowrie exaggerating? Not if the greatness of a novelist stems from his willingness to accept life as he finds it without wishing it into something grand or high falutin'. In Eddie Coyle, the Digger, and Jackie Cogan, Higgins follows the examples of his fellow Irishmen Samuel Beckett and the Brian Moore of *The Lonely Passion of Judith Hearne* (1955); he scuttles the middle-class heroes and bourgeois settings of Dickens and Anthony Trollope in favor of marginal, often lowlife types. Here is Gowrie's salute to Higgins in full. Perhaps its enthusiasm reflects, not Joyce's aesthetic in *A Portrait*, but the *Ulysses* prized by T. S. Eliot for a breadth of vision he defined as classical: "For me [said Gowrie], Higgins is the great classical novelist of the late twentieth century in America. His rivals are John Updike and Saul Bellow, and he differs from them in being wholly uninterested in ideas. This is a classical characteristic. Ideas date. Human situations do not."[12]

Higgins's interest in ideas like entropy and Occam's razor doesn't disqualify him as a classic in Gowrie's sense of the term. For Higgins, ideas are part of life, not an ornament or decoration superadded to it. They're integral to the life he has put himself on a level with. Besides, what price ideas? There are more ideas on a page of Thomas Mann (and in a short paragraph of Robert Musil) than in twenty-five pages of Higgins or Henry James, with whom he has been compared. Yes, Higgins's imagination inclines to lawbreakers. But, to cite James again, lawbreakers were his *donnée*. Whether seen in a workingman's bar or a country club, they stoked both his voracious curiosity and his great interest in human nature. He judged well to build his fictional corpus around them. As he said, the creative process is mysterious (CADS 1, 31), and any creator who slights its offerings would be stupid. Credit him, too, for taking these gifts at face value. His refusal to play scourge or scold helped him produce books that were "very black" (Brady 27). But it also helped him invest his rogues with such immediacy that they shocked readers. This vividness demonstrates a hallmark principle of prose fiction, the value of live action over analysis or explanation. Accolades to him.

In most of the books from his middle and late periods, though, the vividness took forms that puzzled and in some cases angered admirers of the stunning, hard-hitting trio of works, starting with *Eddie Coyle*, that launched his novelistic career. This, Higgins knew: "the people who liked the earlier books . . . disapproved of the longer, middle and later ones" (Brady 27). But he was too modest to add that these books also harbored rewards. These are remarkable, even though some of their detractors ignored them. Listening to the sounds these books make will frame both their rewards and disincentives in a context where they can be fairly judged. Trust your ears. The sensual truth will emerge and the comedy, begin.

Notes

1. Ross Macdonald said Raymond Chandler "wrote like a slumming angel and invested the sun-stopped streets of Los Angeles with a romantic presence"; Tom Nolan, *Ross Macdonald: A Biography* (New York: Scribners, 1999), 321; George V. Higgins, "Preface: A Man of Measured Discontents—John O'Hara and His Losses," *Gibbsville, PA: The Classic Stories*, by John O'Hara, ed. Matthew J. Bruccoli (New York: Carroll & Graf, 1992), 12.

2. George V. Higgins, "All Day Was All There Was," *Arizona Quarterly* 19 (Spring 1963): 13; George V. Higgins, "Something Dirty You Could Keep," *Massachusetts Review* 10 (Autumn 1963): 31–44.

3. Kenneth Millar, "The Inward Eye: A Revaluation of Coleridge's Psychological Criticism," PhD diss., University of Michigan, 1951.

4. George V. Higgins, "The Private Eye as Illegal Hero," *Esquire*, December 1972, 348, 350–1.

5. See also George V. Higgins, *The Sins of The Fathers* (London: Andre Deutsch, 1988), 21–38.

6. Dashiell Hammett, *Red Harvest, The Novels of Dashiell Hammett* (1929; New York: Knopf, 1973), 172; Dashiell Hammett, *The Maltese Falcon* (1930; New York: Random House: Vintage Crime/Black Lizard, 1992), 35.

7. George V. Higgins, "Mass in the Time of War," *Cimarron Review*, September 1969, 79.

8. Raymond Chandler, *The Big Sleep* (1939; New York: Random House; Vintage Crime/Black Lizard, 1992), 8.

9. Raymond Chandler, *The Long Goodbye* (1953; New York: Random House: Vintage Crime/Black Lizard, 1992), 23.

10. William Gaddis, *Carpenter's Gothic* (1985; New York: Penguin, 1986), 241.

11. William Gaddis, *JR* (1975; New York: Penguin, 1993), 3.

12. Grey Gowrie, "Profanity Behind the Tea Parties," *Sunday Telegraph*, 12 November 1989, 18.

Chapter Five

Some Words onna Street

Higgins's classical poise shows itself in language that's appealingly confident, natural, and unforced. At his best, he challenges readers to rethink their preconceived notions about fiction itself. He has also extended critical parameters. His prose is so economical yet lively and sharp, so tightly fitted yet continuously fluid, that it mystifies us; we suspect that there's something wrong with it that we've missed. Yet he's quick to quiet our suspicions. To begin with, his unpublished essay, "Introduction," which is stored at the University of South Carolina's Thomas Cooper Library, says that "the novelist who wrenches his characters around in order to make ideological points or deliver moral lessons disservices the reader" (1). Thomas Wolfe made this mistake. In *On Writing* (1990), Higgins calls him "extremely stupid" (34) because he kept butting into his stories, denying the reader the fun of figuring them out himself.

Fiction-writing, Higgins believes, is an uphill fight; the reader knows from the start that the story he's reading was made up. Herein lies the task Higgins set himself. He had to write stories vivid enough to make the reader suspend his disbelief in their actuality. He goes about this task by depersonalizing himself; he lets the stories tell themselves. We walk alongside his characters; we're seldom ahead of them. We're certainly not allowed to rise above them and look down on them. His belief, "all fiction is gossip, and the best of it is collected by eavesdropping" (OW 121), helps him in two ways. Gossips don't want to change the world; they like it as it is. The next step is logical. The production of good fiction depends upon the art of listening; the fiction writer, having endowed his characters with life, becomes more of a recorder than a creator. Higgins enjoys the role of eavesdropper or snoop. And by doing so, he has also turned an important truth to his—and our—favor. Gossips lower their guard, a condition that helps the wary snoop.

The factual truth gleaned by the snoop usually means less than the truth's impact upon the snoop's feelings. Keats's doctrine of negative capability comes to mind here. Invoking it himself, Keats wrote perfectly about gnats, lambs, and swallows while fighting the tuberculosis that would soon kill him. Replace these barnyard creatures with hot cars fresh from the midnight auto supply, contraband guns, and the screaming rafters of Boston Garden. Yes, the

69

environments where Higgins's books unfold are or were familiar (the Garden no longer exists). But we adjust quickly. The deeper we get into one of his plots, the less outrageous the details become. They needn't be physical. A careful fiction writer won't violate probability by having a character do and say things that clash with his personality. A story must be plausible or the reader, who knows it to be "a pack of lies" (OW 138), will put it down. To build plausibility, the writer must collect and assemble information he accepts the meaning of (OW 145) without bending it in a direction he believes more ethically satisfying. Eddie Coyle is a crook pure and simple. Don't try to make him conform to middle-class morality. You'll be playing his nature false, and the reader will resent you for it.

Higgins conveys plausibility through mood and, mostly, tone, which he crafts as a stylistic vehicle of theme. On this score, he admires Ring Lardner's "tonal savagery," adding, "Lardner was a merciless writer, and those are the best kind" (OW 152). This brutality, no defect, Higgins hails as a blow for freedom. A force for justice, too, it's a function of self-negation. Simultaneously tender and tough, it requires the tact and restraint often associated with modesty. Resist coloring the objective truth with your wishes or beliefs; at the same time, have the courage to present the truth as you see it. Discussing *Cogan's Trade*, D. Keith Mano yokes Higgins's art to his lawyering: "Higgins's approach is evidential. He doesn't judge. He is unassertive as a court stenographer."[1]

Unassertive but not tentative or bland; his descriptions, both bright and exact, have the power to take us wherever he's writing about. They also take us there quickly. Speaking of the opening paragraph of *Eddie Coyle*, Robert B. Parker says, "We are in the story, smack up against it, in fact, with no warning. . . . We are witnessing a story as it unfolds, almost narrationless, entirely dramatized."[2] This suspension of moral judgment has won Higgins artistic points. By not urging his scenes to prearranged moral resolutions, he brings his people to full, sometimes frightening life.

Like everyone else, he *has* opinions and beliefs. But they're trumped in his fiction by his dramatic flair—his ear for speech, his urban evocations, and his superbly controlled images. His belief in authorial exclusion has helped him shape a body of fiction more presentational than tendentious or analytical. A short description in Higgins has more impact than pages of brooding analysis. Though the places his people inhabit can be small, mean, and dangerous, his staging of them calls forth Chekhov's ruefully comic detachment; without any prodding from him, the people both reflect and create their physical milieus. Again like Chekhov, he may start a scene *in medias res*, inviting us to find our own way into it. As heedless of his readers as a good screen actor is of the camera, he may even throw in a reference for verisimilitude's sake we might miss, like the one in *Digger* to ex-NFL quarterback, Y.A. Tittle, who retired in 1964.[3]

He has been refining the art of the eavesdropper. Nearly passive, he writes to find out why rather than to serve notice or make pronouncements. His ability to listen provides a vivid sense of authenticity, all the more vital in novels whose very foundations keep shifting in the treacherous sands of opportunism. But his fine sense of place, his feel for interpersonal dynamics, and his selection, i.e., his knowing *which* materials to include and *where* to put them, all firm up the narrative groundwork. Higgins will bolster a scene with intriguing information he'll either include as a throwaway detail or a prepared statement from a specialist. A marine biologist in *Edgar* discusses the toxic effects of low tides upon municipal water systems (163). To buttress his discussion, Higgins had noted that the marine biologist was developing "systems which incinerate solid waste and treat liquid wastes in such a fashion as to reduce the coliform bacterial count of the discharge to negligible levels" (160).

The canon profits often from the research that delivered such insights. Nor does the research stand as an undigested lump. Very rarely does background detail rout foreground action in Higgins. *The Mandeville Talent* (1991) directs his knowledge of domestic architecture and landscaping to the enterprise of home-buying, including, in passing, tips on seeing through the spiels mouthed by realtors to break down sales resistance.[4] This diligence shores up his career at every phase. *Impostors* (1986) includes a winning description of the preparation and serving of food (114) as well as longer passages, rich in medical detail, that recount both the dangers and treatment of drug abuse (307). A man in *Change of Gravity* is asked, "[I]s there anything you don't know" (353)? The question might have been put to Higgins many times, perhaps even when he was writing his 1997 novel, a work steeped in the lore of golf and golf courses, boats and boatyards, and, as often happens in his work, cars and car dealerships.

Higgins can also question or prod himself in the service of his art. "You have to pay attention in this world, every damned minute. No matter what you're doing" (334), says someone in *Impostors*. Higgins is reminding himself of the importance of being on the watch for illuminating details. Omitting such data from stories that would gain from their inclusion constitutes literary crime for him. It also sheds light on a work ethic that scrutinizes whatever it touches. Carelessness is a trap. Regardless of what you're doing, do it carefully and thoroughly, lest someone notice and fix you good—as you deserve. A politician in *Choice of Enemies* (1984) who knows the reality of appearances explains the great care he must take each time he goes out in public:

> [I]t is not going to be enough if I just throw on a sport coat and a tie and show up at the funeral home. Uh uh. I've got to shower, I've got to blow-dry my hair. I've got to shave neat and put on the aftershave lotion, and I've got to wear a tie and coat that's different from what I wore to Mass this morning. Because if the people who saw me at Mass this morning in my tweed sport coat don't see me at the wake tonight wearing my blue blazer, they are going to say to themselves: "Ray didn't put himself out much for this one, did he now?" And it will be just exactly like I never went at all. (CE 226-7)

As Ray Archambault implies, style and substance often merge. Understanding the high cost of skimping details, Higgins the honest craftsman also tries to look closely to all sides of an issue. This attentiveness pays off. In no time, he'll say enough about a topic to convince readers that it deserves their attention. The topic itself doesn't matter. Chapter Eighteen of *Wonderful Years* goes over the requirements bonding companies impose upon contractors before they'll consider loaning the contractors money. And before setting more than half the action of *Swan Boats* on a luxury liner, Higgins studied shipboard protocol regarding international manifests, food service, and the attire worn by different members of the crew on different occasions; nor will he call a port a window, a bulkhead a wall, or a hatch a window (Swan 39, 42).

His magpie knowledge continues to amaze. Though a character in *Dreamland* doesn't know why the manufacture of a certain kind of paint requires an ingredient called butadiene, Higgins explains why this flammable hydrocarbon helps make synthetic rubber, a point more vital to the book's plot (D 97). Chapter Thirteen of *Outlaws* includes a ballistic report that tells about a specific weapon, its manufacture, and the evidence provided by the bullets fired from it. Later in *Outlaws*, Higgins sends a troupe of classical musicians to the University of Missouri-Kansas City, an appropriate venue for a concert in 1987, the date of the book's release, given UMKC's then blossoming graduate program in music. Sometimes a detail is managed so discreetly that it nearly escapes us (while also making us wonder how much treasure we might have *already* missed). Two vacationers in *Wonderful Years* discover Nell Farley's corpse while they're facing west (255-7), the sundowning direction associated with death in works like E. A. Robinson's "Luke Havergal," John Steinbeck's 1939 *Grapes of Wrath*, and John Fowles's *Magus* (1965).

Concrete references in *A Year or so with Edgar* are also dramatic, even though they may also serve different ends. The following passage from the book uses a run of fashion details to convey a nerd's transformation into a near-swinger, 1970s style:

> I noticed that the pince-nez had been replaced by blue-tinted aviator glasses. I noticed that the short graying hair was no longer short. It had been blown dry. . . . I observed that Franklin was wearing a gold ID bracelet on his right wrist. And that his father's heirloom Hamilton watch had been replaced by a Seiko calculator. (59)

Higgins treatment of such details respects both the reader and the norms of prose narrative. Yes, Higgins is a polymath. But his knowledge isn't intrusive. Rather than flaunting it, he has learned to mete it out wisely, sometimes even invisibly, in the right places. But more is needed to dovetail concrete references into a fiction than a good sense of timing. Knowing that readers enjoy being informed, he has also developed, with his candid voice, a delivery system that makes information both easy and pleasant to take in. He neither talks down nor dumbs down. Since his storytelling *élan* has, in all likelihood, already impressed his readers, he leaves them feeling both well informed and flattered.

They've also had a lesson in good writing. Besides validating a milieu with sensory details, he has also translated feelings into physical events. A feather touch, an eye for the sudden, unlooked for turns in social experience, and an understanding of the uses of repetition brighten his description of a woman's sudden loss of composure in *Penance for Jerry Kennedy*: "Mack . . . looked troubled. . . . She took a small sip of her brandy, but that was one more sip than she planned to take" (54).

A reference can burst forth suddenly. It can also adapt to the conventions of first-person narrative. "It seemed to have become suddenly very cold and damp in the bar; I had a clammy feeling" (120), Jerry Kennedy remarks inwardly when a lunch companion mentions Jerry's ex-wife in *Defending Billy Ryan*. "The clamminess was coming back" (121), Jerry notes minutes later, suffering the distress of sudden entrapment. An alert reader will also connect the redness that flares out on a policeman's neck in *Bomber's Law* (63) to the onset of anger. The reverse also holds. The reader may also decipher the meaning of a physical event that, though anticipated, *doesn't* occur. Before the present-tense action of *Bomber*, Gayle Dell'Appa's politically connected father exiled Harry to a duty station in western Massachusetts to punish him for cheating on Gayle. Harry grazes this episode in conversation with Gayle just as she's carrying a platter of hot chicken to the dinner table. That she drops neither the chicken nor the gravy boat she picks up seconds later bespeaks a rare poise and self-presence. Harry, whose rutting merits him a hot gravy shampoo, is luckier than he knows to have her as a wife. Again, selection, timing, and emphasis have scored Higgins a point from what looks like chance references, helping him stave off the dead hand of explanation and analysis.

I

Higgins's attention to technique hasn't swamped his sense of fun. Playfulness and a flair for repetition put the words cahoots, cahooting, and cahooted on the same page of *Bomber* (269). Elsewhere, the word pranks reveal a Joycean edge. The crook Andy Marr in *Deke Hunter* has parents named Frances and Francis (184). Bernie Morgan's wife and girlfriend in *Choice* both go by Maggie. Characters named Feeley and Farley appear in *Wonderful Years*. Building on the pattern, the book also includes characters with either the first or last names of Wilson, Wiltse, Whipple, and Wixton. Higgins's boldest name patterning, though, comes in *The Patriot Game* (1982), which includes the FBI agent Peter Riordan and one Reardon, Chairman of the Ways and Means Committee for the Commonwealth of Massachusetts (Bernie Morgan's job in Higgins's next book, *Choice)*. In a bodacious stroke, Higgins brings the two together. Though the meeting is held in Reardon's office, it shows the ex-marine Riordan riding herd over his near-namesake. The rout gives us pause. If Reardon's defeat on his own turf calls forth the hierarchical thinking drilled into Higgins as a boy (a bishop will also put down a monsignor in the book), it also shows his urge to keep testing himself. He remains a man on the move.

His 1972 statement in *Esquire*, "The P[rivate]. I[nvestigator]. is an invariably urban character; the only time you will find him in the woods is . . . to chase somebody else who has escaped the City" (348), backs his denial that he wrote crime novels (Williams 205). Virtually all of *Wonderful Years* and *Victories* take place far from the urban underworld he's usually linked with. Neither book is plain spoken, muslin textured in the Norman Rockwell vein, or written along rustic lines. Of the two, *Victories* reflects more of a rural outlook, both describing the toil of surviving in the backwoods (349) and celebrating, in long, meandering sentences, the beauties of western Vermont near Lake Champlain, where Hank Briggs works as a game warden. In Chapter Two, Hank inspects a barn with the sound of "swallows rustling overhead" (20-1). The ambitious next chapter recounts the effects of the post-Civil War collapse of Vermont's wool trade; traces the history of the farmhouse that became, by steps, an IGA store; and lists the items (e.g., "power-hand tools, sturdy clothing, pharmaceuticals" [24-5]) found on the shelves. Some local color is also filled in. The merchants of the fictional town where the IGA stands, Occidental, have learned to get along, some of them chatting daily in the same lunch room --not that they'd admit that these chats bring them back every day--while also steering clear of each other's customers during business hours. Governing this delicate dynamic is the pretense, set forth in an understated New England way, that the town's merchants never raid each other's client pool.

Hank Briggs's job as a guardian of the local wildlife, besides giving rise to some lyrical descriptions of the nearby lakes and mountains, offers insight into the protection and preservation of rural property; the carcasses of crows killed by dive-bombing owls must be removed quickly lest they attract raccoons, who will also overturn trashcans scrounging for food and thus vex the locals—who live miles from the Mafiosi of Providence or Boston.

Again shifting venues, Higgins writes in *Bomber's Law* and *Swan Boats* other paradigmatic tales of complex people navigating complex relationships. He also weds this subject matter to an astonishing command of the resources of the language. This gift, which distinguished his work from the start, takes many forms. First, his knowledge that prose driven by active verbs both moves quickly and generates drive explains the presence in one paragraph of *City on a Hill* (1975) of the words bounced, whacked, and swooped (8). Active verbs energize his prose in places where energy is called for; some bulldozers in *Choice* "snarled and roared" (22) over land being leveled prior to the pouring of tons of cement.

Higgins's inventiveness with verbs takes different forms. *The Mandeville Talent* includes chamber, as in placing a shell in the breech of a shotgun, and the compound verbs ping-ponged and fine-tooth-combed (5, 119, 194). *Sandra*

Nichols (21) and *Change of Gravity* (85) recycle this bonding technique with chainsaw and cold-turkey. Even a passive-verb construction in Higgins can make you gasp. Coming, intriguingly, in an extended description of the interplay of colors and textures in a home, a paragraph opens, "The couch was slipcovered in bright yellow" (I 73). The sentence's vibrant closing image carries forward the excitement created by its inventive main verb. Despite this passive-voice construction, the sentence reads better than the active-voiced, "The couch had a yellow slipcover." The neologism, slipcovered, highlights boldly and originally the sentence's—and the couch's—leading attribute.

Irony builds from sentence mechanics in *Penance*: "Among Henry's many excellent personal qualities is a broad streak of treachery" (11). It can also be thematic. A prosecutor in *Outlaws* accuses a defendant of committing crimes so brutal that only a madman could have thought them up (132). Later, though, the prosecutor asks the defendant's ex-girlfriend to marry him. But he frames his proposal in terms as mad as those he found motivating her ex-lover's crimes; Christina Walker must wait five years to wed Terry Gleason, spending every New Year's Eve alone and eating Saturday night dinners by herself in front of the TV before Gleason will feel ready to leave his small son.

Symbolism is another poetic device Higgins will use both to define and deepen a sexual tie. Let *Trust* serve as an example. Earl Beale's plan to share a Thanksgiving turkey with Penny Slate gets shipwrecked by her boss's offer of $15,000 to weekend with him in New York. Adrift and feeling abandoned in the apartment he shares with Penny, Earl sees the turkey they had set out to thaw discolor and soften as it also begins to stink. Looking at and smelling the rancid turkey spurs an insight in Earl. He is the turkey. The recognition saps so much of his vim that he has to lie down. In the next paragraph, he reaches under the iron frame of the bed he shares with Penny and recoils from the unpleasantness of touching the dust balls lodged there. This shock represents another turning point for him. Four chapters and a week later he recalls the dust balls' "furry and threatening" sensation (T 185). Though flimsy, weightless, and gossamer-like, the dust balls have clinched in Earl's mind the decay and loss of his hopes that he both saw and smelled in the rotting turkey, once a symbol to him of warmth and connection.

Thematic heft in Higgins often stems from his ability to combine and recombine symbolic motifs. An example comes in a reference in Chapter Seventeen of *Trust* to the "trail of paper that goes everywhere they roam, just like Mary's little lamb" (195), left by Penny's Thanksgiving weekend date exactly two months after their New York trip (191). No frill, the carefully thought-out detail both invokes the woolen dust balls that menaced Earl in Chapter Twelve and reminds us that Penny's real name in Mary (5). Earl's life plummets after his glimpse of the moldering turkey tells him that his sad, lonely Thanksgiving has set him on a downward slope. Mary will always desert her little lamb in favor of brighter prospects. His plunge accelerates with his writing Penny a note on the backside of a series of canceled checks. Not only is he a canceled check. His action also shows that things used for purposes other than their intended ones always spells trouble in Higgins, who clinches the point by having Earl fill the note, short as it is, with lies.

The symbolism that moves so much freight so gracefully in *Trust* recalls another writer who infused his portrayals of sexual bonding with a great deal of symbolism. The killing or subduing of animals in D.H. Lawrence's "Love on the Farm," *Women in Love,* and "The Fox," like Higgins's decomposing turkey, all chart key moments for lovers. They also invite another comparison. Like Oliver Mellors of *Lady Chatterley's Lover,* the forest warden Hank Briggs of *Victories* protects natural growing things. Earl Beale and Jerry Kennedy both follow Baxter Dawes, Walter Morel and his son Paul of *Sons and Lovers* by going to pieces after losing their women.

Sexually charged symbolism in Higgins can also remind us, as Henry Green did in *Back* (1946), that life differs from any printed text; a symbolic pattern in a story might shipwreck the silly reader who applies it to life. This warning can come indirectly. The title story of *The Easiest Thing in the World* (2004) includes one Milton Mallus, whose last name, a fusion of mallet and phallus, yokes him to male authority and the strong punishing male. Yet the story's action belies this bond. Prized by his girlfriend, Barbara Harkness Kendrick, for his "considerateness, thoughtfulness . . . and . . . decency" (3), he also gets murdered. Did Barbara's beauty, outstanding enough to merit three citations (2, 9) either kill Mallus or prime him for the kill? The American writers Hemingway, Chandler, and Mary Gaitskill connect beauty to power. Beauty in all three writers grants its lucky possessors an extra share of pleasure and wealth, often at the expense of a male intimate; husbands of stunning beauties die in Hemingway's "Macomber" and in Chandler's *Big Sleep* and *Long Goodbye* (in Gaitskill, the man dishes out the woe).

Long Goodbye also reminds us that its author was often praised for charging classic British syntax with an American vocabulary. Without discrediting this feat, I must note that Higgins's work reflects a more thorough grounding in the resources of English prose than Chandler's. Nor does the array of tropes found in his work dissolve in the truth that he wrote nearly five times as much as Chandler. *Style vs. Substance* includes the following aphorism: "Old political alliances, however close and personal, tend to resemble old love affairs, more suitable for nostalgic reflection than for revival" (184-5). A paragraph in this 1984 political treatise begins with the epigram, "Boston is to envy as Chicago is to wind"; it ends with the still nastier, "In Boston, no good fortune is official until somebody has urinated on it" (141). Paradox takes root in the canon with Jerry "Digger" Doherty, a thug who's also a worried protective father of four school-age children he takes to the beach on his days off. But the paradox drives still deeper. The priest-brother of this ex-con, thief, and fence reappears as a bishop in *Patriot Game.*

Higgins uses simile less often than Chandler and Ross Macdonald. But he uses it well. The sentence, "Andrew's anger came up the back of his neck like a flag" (D 160), conveys his preference for show over tell. In *Mandeville Talent,* simile again conveys distress in this rendering of the force of a December gale: the gale "whined down . . . like a meat saw, nothing personal but well-adapted to separating joints and ribs" (5); nature's indifference to humanity reduces us to slabs of meat in a butcher's shop. Significantly, the sentence also includes a metaphor, which, happily, occurs in the sentence's main verb ("whined"), where it packs the most force. Though not a metaphorical writer, Higgins could use metaphor capably and comfortably. He certainly didn't avoid it. A man given to sarcasm in *Edgar* has "a tongue on him that you could use to strip paint" (68). More grandly, metaphor swathes *The Rat on Fire* (1981), some of which unfolds in a rat-ridden apartment building (rightly called a "rathole" [89]). The building's tenants fall into two camps. The minority, mostly jobless, toss trash out of their windows and sometimes even tear out their bathroom plumbing for resale. The majority belong to the working poor. They are losing heart because the dominant society lied to them. No matter how much they toil, their debts keep mounting.

The rats that have been infesting their building stand as a metaphor for the novel itself. Carriers of typhus and syphilis, the rat plagues slum dwellers everywhere; it's hard to imagine a ghetto creature more feared and hated. Even the owner of the building under discussion has been avoiding its cellar— advisedly, the place picked by arsonist Leo Proctor to ignite some gasoline-soaked rats which he'll then slip into the building's heating ducts. The building itself, though sadly neglected, is structurally sound (RF 55-6), signaling Higgins's fondness for heritage architecture (see also CG, Chapter Twenty-Five, 404-25). That it can net its owner more cash as a burnt-out husk than as a living space for people denotes the wrongness of the American city. Even the arsonist hired to torch the building won't enter its cellar without a flashlight. It makes sense that he fears entrapment. Both his fear and his felonious mission tally with the maze symbolism that Baudelaire, Conan Doyle, and T.S. Eliot all deployed in their portraits of the western metropolis. The association of mazes with rats belittles us all. Perhaps it panicked Leo Proctor. The singular noun, rat, used in the title of the novel featuring him, stands for all rats, just as he fears dying from a rat's bite.

Other stylistic devices operating on a smaller scale also show the training and care that distinguish the Higgins books. The phrase, "that battalion of blithe brats" (DBR 219), while perhaps grazing the extravagance of tabloid prose, transmits Higgins's fondness for alliteration. A more skillfully wrought verbal cluster, from the *Hudson Review* story (Winter, 1983-84), "Ducks and Other Citizens," "the broadback flats of salt" (SF 175), joins consonance to assonance. Another story in *Sins of the Father*, "Bliss," uses synecdoche. Three sentences after introducing "this guy in a cheap sports coat," Higgins has "the cheap sports coat," not its wearer, hand the story's narrator a piece of paper.

Higgins's language training comes forth, too, in these examples of litotes found in both *Kennedy for the Defense* ("I shot a hole in the woodwork. . . . It didn't do his eardrum any good [224]) and *Defending Billy Ryan* ("the complaining witnesses [whose testimony could sink Jerry's client] were in the federal jug . . . which did him [namely, the client] no harm" [16]). But the figure of speech from classical rhetoric that Higgins likes the most is zeugma. It appears in work from each of his decades as a published novelist. Andy Marr of *Deke Hunter* (1976) wears "a green blazer . . . and a bored expression" (187). A reporter in *Edgar* (1979) has "a bloody Maria and an argument with a . . . young man" (55). A lawyer in *Rat* (1981) wears a "brown suit and a stern expression" (81). The figure returns, sartorial context and all, in *A Change of Gravity* (1997), when a blue-suited lawyer displays "a narrow maroon knit tie . . . and a worried expression" (378). Heed these examples. Any writer who invites similarities that have escaped us, no matter how farfetched, enlarges our sense of the possible.

Even more prevalent in the canon, though, than zeugma is the parallel construction, which Higgins builds, as Hammett did in *Maltese Falcon*, by putting a sentence's active main verb immediately after its pronoun subject, He (viz.,"He looked. . . . He poked. . . . He held" [*Falcon* 91]), to depict the steadiness and thoroughness with which a professional works. Now the pro may be a crook (RF 114), whose slow precision, patience, and attention to detail all boost his chances to succeed. Even a loser like Earl Beale of *Trust* acts with composure and presence of mind while setting up a blackmail scheme (T 32-3). The parallel construction serves Higgins's purposes and aims. In *Digger* (1973) it captures the ritual-like decorum governing a Mafiosi dinner (148). Again using the feast or meal as its context in *Victories*, it voices Higgins's fascination with the process of preparing dishes, i.e., knowing both which foods to serve and which of them tastes best where: "Whipple poured Worcestershire sauce into the pool of ketchup and mixed the combination with his fork. Then he put the pork chop into the mixture, turning it so that it was coated on both sides. Then he spooned the hash-brown potatoes into the puddle of sauce and stirred them vigorously" (V 32).

II

His belief in man's basic dishonesty (and maybe also depravity) (Bannon 26) prompted Higgins to write about crimes performed by chronic lawbreakers. He also punctures the shams we hide behind to lighten the plod of daily life. The victories won in *Victories* come at a high cost, and the golden age the alcoholic mental patient Nell Farley rhapsodizes about in *Wonderful Years* (131) probably never happened. Had it existed as she claims, she'd not have turned to the bottle, and her husband Ken would have stayed with her. But the tough-minded Higgins will also buckle to sentimentality, going soft and soppy about things he never knew first hand, if they existed at all. His use of the verb "hoover' (WY 205), his reference to the "grille" of a car (T 25), and his citing a Boston lawyer who had been "invalided home" (like Conan Doyle's Watson and Christie's Hastings) after losing an arm in World War II (CG 43) harks to a culture even more august than that of the old-stock New Englanders who set the standard of breeding and behavior for the Brockton-born Catholic writer.

This standard he didn't buy full cloth. The Wills clan of *Dreamland* is so elite that the blazers and white flannels they wear at family dinners might as well have come from Bond Street or Burlington Arcade; in fact, a Wills spent most of Hitler's War in England. The family's traditional Christmas includes English customs, trappings, and food. Yet both adultery and crime have stained the Wills dynasty. Perhaps there are other blemishes. According to Higgins, the book's narrator, Compton Wills, the family's youngest offshoot, is "probably deranged" (CADS 2, 4).

Daniel Compton Wills's mental problems, though, don't distract Higgins any more than his pedigree, though the two may be related. Higgins anchors himself in specifics whether they be pork chops and hash browns (V 32) or lobster salad and chilled white wine (T 185). Life's diversity and sensuous vitality stirs his genius for recovering those special qualities that impart uniqueness. At any time, this erstwhile denizen of Boston's underworld will delight in small particulars, the observation of which usually belongs to women writers like Eudora Welty, Penelope Fitzgerald, and Anita Brookner. More needs to be said about Higgins's feminine streak. Co-existing with his trademark flair for crime and criminals is a tenderness, a love of beautiful things, and an appreciation of human bonds, particularly within the family. In the Jerry Kennedy books, the female imperatives of warmth and belonging rout the male ones of competition and self-advancement.

Making the tension sing is his genius for curating the oddments of his and our mental furniture. Admittedly, some of this gear occupies more space inside *his* head than ours, proving that the writer who wants to hold his readers' attention must stick to what he knows. Not only do lawyers play big parts in most of his books. Legal terms like durance vile (PJK 91), allocution (O 156), and *duces tecum* (WY 127) lace their conversations both in and out of the courtroom. And maybe fog it a bit, too; much of Chapter Seventeen of *Wonderful Years* (174-84), which unfolds in a room adjoining a federal attorney's office, consists of shoptalk more interesting to lawyers and their acolytes than to outsiders.

But the law is only one of many strands that a Higgins novel will play out before combining and recombining them with others. In *On Writing* (1990) he says, "All writing that intrigues intelligent readers . . . is news" (33). Readers who spot features of their interior landscapes in a story will keep turning pages. One of the joys of Higgins's fiction comes from recognizing how wide-awake and responsive he is to the inner spaces we share with his people. By recording the changes, the pastimes, and the talk that define lives on the move, he gives his work a stylish, impromptu intelligence. Higgins maps popular culture with the same witty flair as Philip Roth, Salman Rushdie, and Sam Shepard. Political handlers in *The Agent* stress the importance of "staying on message" (262). Like the worrisome cholesterol that's discussed in *Digger* (149-50) and the NEXIS,

LEXIS website a woman in *Penance* rigs to her computer (40), the Julio Iglesias concert attended by four characters in *Wonderful Years* tethers the novels to a shared reality.

This reality spreads wide enough to swathe many psyches and sensibilities. A coded message that baseball fans might enjoy comes in *Victories*. Former Red Sox pitcher Hank Briggs probably named his son Ted after Bosox Hall of Famer Ted Williams. The *last* name given to both father and son by Higgins squares with that of the home field of the Detroit Tigers, for whom Hank pitched after being traded to Detroit, where, decades earlier, baseball great Ty Cobb thrilled hometown fans. The point deserves mention for two reasons: a major character in *Victories* is called *Ed* Cobb, and a Mike "Pinky" *Higgins* played third base for both the Detroit Tigers and the Red Sox. Sports trivia addicts will also take special joy in spotting casual, yet accurate, references to ex-NFL quarterback Norm Snead (CT 29) and former big-league catcher, the bespectacled Clint Courtney (JDH 102).

There's plenty in Higgins's fictional world to charm all readers, giving it broad-based appeal. Besides finding room for Shakespeare (e.g., BL 114, 250), it also quotes some of the songs from *Kiss Me Kate*, Cole Porter's 1948 musical rendition of *The Taming of the Shrew* (BL 20, Easiest 67). New Englanders will find captivating landmarks in Waterford, Massachusetts, venue for parts of *Impostors*, *Outlaws*, and *Wonderful Years*. The stores and streets, shopping malls and law enforcement systems, of this fictional town create a personality that fuses aspects of the New England temperament. Higgins also chose the town's name carefully. Though no Waterford exists in Massachusetts, towns called Waterford both in Ireland and elsewhere in the United States have a pleasing familiarity that justified Higgins's annexing the name for a generic satellite city of Boston.

III

The trim, clean-running folkloric prose of Higgins's first three novels startled readers. These dialogue-driven books rivet on characters who flout accepted standards of civilized living and discourse. Higgins's secret for making us care about these hoods? Authorial exclusion; as he said in his Afterword to James Ross's neglected 1940 masterpiece, *They Don't Dance Much*, "the primary concern of the novelist" is "to let the reader find out for himself."[5] Higgins not only faced the truth of Boston's underworld; he also framed his insights in dialogue to put us on hard, non-judgmental terms with it. The terms hold. Even though his ear is flawless, his unpretentious manner makes his prowess easy to miss. Dialogue moves the action while also compelling us with its content, cadence, and flow. It sounds like real, breathing human speech. We have to be impressed; it's harder for a writer to be simple than to be clever.

Higgins characters who schmooze in cars and taverns without settling any major issues prove that correctly managed talk needn't advance a plot or develop an idea. Its value in Higgins comes from the speed with which it builds a mood or captures the vigor of Boston crimespeak. The method governing this gritty, sometimes brutal talk is modest. Rather than over-explaining, selling an idea, or milking material for shock value, dialogue in Higgins provides access to the woes and sporadic joys of his people. Syntax and word choice lend psychological accuracy to his accessions. The people may blurt out the first thing that comes to mind without organizing their thoughts grammatically or even consecutively. Also remarkable is the way this edgy, nervous talk includes the elisions, omissions, and trailings-off of real speech.

But words can also be added as well as being smothered or snipped. Jerry "Digger" Doherty's statement to his brother, "I feel like somebody kicked me in the guts, is how I felt" (DG 82), ends with a four-word phrase that, though redundant, has a savor and intimacy that warrant its inclusion in the sentence. Besides sounding natural, the phrase, no chunk of dead wood, evokes the Digger's background, life style, and social status. E.A. Levenston would call the sentence that includes the phrase an example of right dislocation. His sharp 1981 essay, "Literary Dialect in George V. Higgins's 'Judgment of Deke Hunter,'" still the most rigorous study of dialogue in the canon, cites his man's "extraordinary feel for the way human relationships are revealed through speech." The "deviant utterances" that lend color and sting to *Deke Hunter* include parataxis, and anacoluthon, of which the pseudo-cleft syntactic pattern of right dislocation forms a sub-category.[6]

These units take shape inside Higgins's head. When he advises the aspiring writer in the first chapter of *On Writing* to read his/her prose aloud, he's invoking common knowledge, i.e., that prose depends as much as poetry does upon rhythm. The writer of prose fiction *can* correct mistakes by reading his/her work aloud (OW 86). Though the narrative passages in Higgins make different sounds on the page than dialogue, he models all of his prose on direct speech. He lets us know it, too. The word, "Mister," is always spelled out. Terminal-degree holders are called "Doctor" (D 95, CE 173). A young lawyer in *Wonderful Years* full of conviction and go-by-the-book rectitude, calls herself "Ms. [Gilda] Bostock" (e.g. 185). People of all social and educational levels use contractions while talking because it's convenient, fully understandable, and natural sounding. Higgins carries this practice further than most writers. He elides "more than" to 'more'n" (D 134, WY 106, MT 111), contracts "I would have" to "I'd've" (O 49, WY 106), shrinks "without" to "'thout" (CG 21), and compresses "don't you" to' 'chou" (CG 405).

Shortening is one of his favorite stylistic devices. In the sentence from *Digger*, "It's tonight I'd be worried about, I was you" (3), the comma replaces the word, if. A comma replaces the preposition, for, in "Didn't register, the draft" (O 24). Sometimes there's no comma; Chapter Twenty-Two of *Impostors* begins with somebody saying, "The truth [of] the matter is" (173). A preposition is missing from the sentence, "Listen [to] the tapes, if you wanna" (BL 19). Elsewhere, a comma stands for two words, as in, "we're prolly all gonna get blown up [in the], nuclear holocaust" (O 200). An apostrophe in Higgins can do the work of a comma. It voices Nell Farley's confusion and regret in *Wonderful Years* when she refers tearily to "my hus' band" (19). This midword pause, perhaps unique in Higgins, harks to Anglo-Saxon verse as well as to moderns like David Jones and James Dickey. But the practice of omitting a word or words to tighten a rhetorical unit could have come to Higgins from his fellow Bay Stater, Emily Dickinson. Here are the closing lines of "The Chariot" (J.712):

> Since then 'tis centuries . . .
> I first surmised the horses' heads
> Were [pointing] toward eternity.

A stylistic flourish can come from anywhere. At its best, Higgins's conversational idiom has the same ground rhythm as Hammett's objective realism. By stringing together sentences of cadence and length without trying to join them, Higgins lets them develop their own connections. Nor does the temporary lack of such links signal slackness or neglect. The two speakers in the following passage from *Bomber* resemble actors in an absurdist play who are pretending to have forgotten their lines:

> "I'm not following you," Dell'Appa said.
> "What?" Brennan said.
> "I don't get it," Dell'Appa said.
> "Don't get what?" Brennan said. "What the hell're you talking about?"
> "What they hell'm I talking about?" Dell'Appa said. What the hell *you're* talking about is what the hell I'm talking about."
> "I don't get it," Brennan said. (BL 11)

Like Samuel Beckett, Higgins may be enacting, in this passage, an interest in states of nonlanguage, nonconsciousness, and consciousness as forms of comedy. Bob Brennan and Harry Dell'Appa are waiting in a car for Short Joe Mossi's brother to walk past them en route to work. To pass the time, they look for topics to discuss. But without success; as has been seen, their partnership is badly strained. They're nearly out of the good will they need to dispense common humanity to each other.

Their loss of patience and politeness is conveyed in part by conversational shifts and stoppages. We can't be surprised; a writer who relies on dialogue as much as Higgins will lean heavily upon the conventions of the stage. The purpose of the following passage from *Outlaws* would otherwise escape us. In it, Higgins seems to be giving information that's both unnecessary and even harmful to sentence flow: "She pulled a cigarette out of the pack and dropped the pack back into her bag. She reached with her left hand for the amber glass ashtray on the table next to her and pulled it nearer" (O 176). The passage does raise questions, since it disrupts the rhythm of a tense discussion. But its resemblance to the famous Pinter pause earns it a second look. No void, the passage creates a silence meant to be filled by the weight of what preceded it. The torrent of talk released by Deke Hunter in Chapter Eighteen of *Judgment* in response to his wife's anxiety about his long absences from home constitutes a different kind of silence. In fact, this long-winded dodge fits Pinter's definition of speech as a stratagem to cover nakedness.

Deke's evasiveness with Andrea was elegantly foreshadowed. The previous chapter began with him "naked in bed" (190) with his girlfriend Madeleine and ended with him saying to her, "I'm not telling" (196). He may be hiding from himself, this corporal in the state police who keeps putting off his sergeant's exam, an impression that builds early in Chapter Eighteen with his answer to Andrea's question, "Where were you last night?" (197). That answer, "When's last night?" (197) marks but one of several evasions he sends her way, Trust and honesty is draining from her marriage, Andrea sees, and she can't stanch the flow.

Another Pinteresque motif shifts mood in Chapter Eleven of *Choice*, in which a Boston journalist stops to refuel his motorcycle at a backwoods gas station. Unluckily for him, the station is manned by a homicidal maniac. Though commonplace, Leo Rosen's purpose for pulling into Roger Knox's Cities Service soon discloses the menace Pinter sees pervading the ordinary. A few minutes at the station floods Leo with the fear that Roger is going to kill him (CE 91). Which Roger *will* try to do; Leo is still in intensive care at book's end, having been put there after Roger's De Soto rammed the same Kawasaki that brought the two men together months before.

This Pinteresque foreshadowing invokes similar patterns in Higgins. Antiphonal voices bring to life a conversation between a glib lawyer and a working-class beautician in Chapter Eight of *Wonderful Years*. Estelle Stoddard's later outmaneuvering of sleek Martin Sands over dinner and the HIV virus she soon infects him with resolve the vocal counterpoint in a dark major chord. The dinner date, like the scene at the Boston hair stylist's shop where Sands and Estelle met, hews to the familiar curve of dialogue—or duologue; Estelle and Sands talk without interruption. But *Wonderful Years* has already varied this standard formula. Chapter Five showed four people talking together, which is much harder work for an author to manage; Chapter Twenty-One of *Choice* consists largely of a three-person conversation; introducing still another variation. Fugue has many uses in Higgins's hands. Chapters Two and Three of *Rat* counterpoints two seemingly unrelated two-man conversations that will later join.

Higgins's devotion to dialogue ("Higgins regards dialogue as the essential key to character," said H. M. Ruppersburg in 1978 [237]) taught him other ways to structure his work musically. Counterpoint builds from inter-cutting in

Judgment. The book's twelfth chapter, called "Part of Charlie's Report," dealt with Deke's marital woes. These intensify in Chapter Thirteen, which describes a dinner party in which it's drunkenly let drop that most of the Hunters' home appliances—dishwasher, fridge, record player—are giving out. Depleted by his affair with Madeleine, Deke's wage packet has nothing left in it for home maintenance. This disclosure comes at a crucial stage, the last chapter of Part Three of *Judgment,* which is also a time when Deke and Andrea are supposed to be having fun. The flat, matter-of-fact title of Chapter Fourteen, "The Rest of Charlie's Report," clashes with the anxiety that ended the previous chapter and with it, for added impact, the book's disturbing third part.

Fugue enhances the action immediately. In order to save on a motel room, Deke had made love to Madeleine in his in-laws' unheated summer cabin. By the end of Chapter Seventeen, Deke's evasiveness and cheapskating spells out his inferiority to *both* her and Andrea. The action of Chapter Eighteen, which follows a motel tryst with Madeleine, marks his moral nadir. Good compositional judgment develops the point. Dramatic momentum demands that Deke's failure with Andrea follow the depiction of his sorry behavior with Madeleine; his home matters more than the motel where he trysted with his girlfriend.

The start of Chapter Eighteen drops him between two major defeats. Yet the chapter's toneless, bare-bones title, "Things as They Become," mutes the stress overtaking him. It also sounds like the title of a children's book. The novel has moved to a different part of the musical scale. Deke, who earns less than Madeleine, would flop as a businessman and, stalled in the rank of Corporal, he hasn't fared much better as a Massachusetts State trooper, either. He's childish, an apt subject for kiddie-lit, in his insistence upon getting his way, regardless of the consequences. Having once flouted an order from his baseball coach, he now both cheats on his wife and imposes on her a living standard far inferior to what she enjoyed before meeting him. It's no wonder that her parents fought the marriage. Perhaps the chapter titles of *The Judgment of Deke Hunter* echo their judgment along with signaling the dearth of *his.* Resolving the plot in a shrill minor chord, the book's off-key-sounding chapter titles explain, finally, that the hunter has been hunted out, discovered, and found wanting.

Narrative economy forms a different counterpoint in *Penance for Jerry Kennedy.* The Jerry of *Kennedy for the Defense* (1980) spent little time on the page with clients, presumably because his home mattered more to him than his work. *Penance* (1985) modifies this scenic distribution, using a technique Higgins might have invented. Jerry will summarize a client's office visit, dwelling on the main points and thus stabilizing narrative focus. For immediacy's sake, his summaries come in conversations held later the same day with his wife, Mack. This technique wins Higgins a bonus. Besides fending off narrative sprawl, it sets forth information while also conveying some of the texture and depth of the Kennedys' marriage.

It could have delivered still more snap had Higgins blocked his "Irish tendency to carry all things to extremes" (PS 194). Certain passages in *Penance* call for the relief provided by inter-cutting. The spate of directly reported speech used to describe Jerry's sessions with his clients leaves us awash in verbiage. Higgins might have felt adrift, too. He shelved his invention for a long time and, when he revived it, in Chapter Eight of *Mandeville Talent*, he halved a conversation between directly reported speech and a discussant's recounting of it--again to his wife later that day.

The absence of swear words in this chapter (MT 76-86) might puzzle readers of Higgins's other work who, logically enough, are waiting for invective to fly from the page and grab them by the throat. Steve Owenby is one of these readers. In 1976, he found Higgins's dialogue "filthy . . . and pretentiously florid" (1303). Following suit, a nameless reviewer in *New Statesman* minced in 1982, "The characters in *The Patriot Game* spend a large proportion of the novel trying to outdo one another in seedy volubility." Back on our shores, Mano objected in 1984 to the cursing in Higgins in more general, sanitized terms: "No one talks quite as his people talk. They're all too witty and never, ever, reticent."[7]

The verbal restraint that Mano couldn't find in *Choice* abounds in *Mandeville Talent* and several other Higgins late books. The difference between a *Choice* or a *Patriot's Game* and a *Talent* impinges upon character and event. Both the subject matter under discussion and the discussants in Chapter Eight of *Talent* rule out profanity. To intrude it would violate Higgins's belief in authorial exclusion. A reader familiar with the characters driving the chapter would recoil had one of them cursed. Their cursing would have betrayed shoddy judgment and technique, Higgins having put words in their mouths. Even more rankling, such a flub would denote Higgins's distrust of the speaker. Here's the big disincentive. A character his author distrusts isn't worth reading about.

But the same complaint can't be made about the hoods and party hacks in *Patriot's Game* and *Choice*. In these novels and, most notably, the first three that Higgins published, obscenities spill out of the characters. To stifle or sugarcoat them would damage the books' credibility. Robert McNeil and William Cran endorsed the vitality of gamy speech when they quoted Walt Whitman's desire for a dictionary that "will give us all the words that exist in use, the bad words as well as any." Like Higgins, Whitman took life on its own terms, positing an America that glories in the dynamics of linguistic variety: "Many of the slang words are our best; slang words among fighting men, gamblers, thieves, are powerful words. . . . The appetite of the people in these States . . . is for unhemmed latitude, coarseness, directness, live epithets, expletives."[8]

The diversity and racy energy displayed by Higgins demand this talk. Why choke it? Isn't language the medium through which members of a group both make themselves and their meanings known to one another? As Higgins shows, their exchanges needn't be aggressive. The obscenities in his work aren't only functional; they're also free of sexuality. None of Higgins's dialogue could inflame the reader. Nor is there an erotic scene in the whole canon. Knowing that his profanity-rife dialogue might shock some readers, he took special care to leach it of erotic content: "They [the obscenities in his books] are used as emphasis, and stress, and a means of showing that the speaker is being very serious about what he has to say and is not a man to be trifled with" (Brady 55).

Barbara Bannon had already discussed the unintrusiveness of the salty speech in Higgins: "You get so you don't even hear it any more" (26), she said in 1973. So smoothly does profanity blend into character and attitude that it becomes thematic. Rather than offending us, it brightens our admiration of Higgins's courage to treat roughnecks and their rough ways honestly. His discretion boosts our admiration still more. His ongoing practice of banishing oaths nearly completely from narration distances him from them. Invisibly, he has aligned himself with his readers, neutralizing, and, in a sense, precluding their objections. His understanding that profanity sometimes rankles and his efforts to draw its sting fuse as a technical triumph. He recounts speech that he tastefully avoids using himself; recounting it fully and accurately is part of his job. Oddly, Peter Lewis, writing in 1981, stands nearly alone in crediting Higgins's ability to hold his poise while writing dialogue that conveys desperation, often of criminals scrabbling for freedom and even survival. Higgins, for Lewis—and for us—has lifted "the colloquial and the foul-mouthed to the level of abrasive eloquence" (640).

Notes

1. D. Keith Mano, "Boston Laconic," *National Review*, 7 June 1974, 655.

2. Robert B. Parker, "Introduction," George V. Higgins, *The Easiest Thing in the World*, vii.

3. George V. Higgins, *The Digger's Game* (New York: Knopf, 1973), 119.

4. George V. Higgins, *The Mandeville Talent* (New York: Henry Holt/A John Macrae Book, 1991), 220-2.

5. George V. Higgins, "Afterword," James Ross, *They Don't Dance Much* (1940; Carbondale and Edwardsville, IL: Southern Illinois University Press, 1975), 301.

6. E.A. Levenston, "Literary Dialect in George V. Higgins's 'Judgment of Deke Hunter,'" *English Studies*, 62 (1981), 358, 368.

7. Steve Owenby, "Adam and Eve-12," *National Review*, 26 November 1976, 1303; "A Foot in the Ground," *New Statesman*, 13 August 1982, 22; D. Keith Mano. "Getting Better All the Time," 18 May 1984, 51.

8. Robert McNeil and William Cram, *Do You Speak American?* (New York: Doubleday: Nan A. Talese, 2001), 14-15.

Chapter Six

The Street Talks Back

Higgins pronounced often on the art of fiction. He discussed it during interviews, taught it at Boston University, and, in *On Writing*, wrote a book about it. But does his practice square with his preachments? The question deserves a close look. Himself the writer of a treatise on style, Herbert Spencer wrote dreadful prose. The author of *The Tragic Muse* famously dismissed most of the Victorian novels he read as "great baggy monsters," and that doyenne of deconstruction, Susan Sontag, wrote, in *The Volcano Lover* (1992), a novel dense with plot, anecdote, and closure.

M.J. Bruccoli judged well to note "Higgins's extraordinary skill with American speech and dialogue" (Easiest, ix). This skill, it again needs saying, rests upon authorial self-erasure. Higgins's believed that any writer of good dialogue must negate himself before becoming someone else; only by suppressing his syntax and vocabulary along with his politics can the fiction writer do justice to somebody else's psyche. Thus speech in Higgins can be nasty, pop-surreal, and both funny and frightening. To William Vesterman, it's a physical event, not just an auditory one; it creates a multi-sensory space we settle into and inhabit. In 1987, Vesterman described Higgins's technique in the opening paragraph of *Eddie Coyle* as an amalgam of tone, gesture, and the unspoken. From this blend, Vesterman says, arises "the sound of a certain kind of thinking out loud . . . until even incomplete sentences make sense" (226). This insight has merit. A Higgins book often feels as if it's being told by a player in the events taking place on the page. What we hear may either fall short of the truth or twist the truth. No lapse or miscue, the part that's withheld or warped thrusts the reader into the picture, where he lives the story rather than being told about it.

This same immediacy makes Bruce Desilva wince. Reviewing *At End of Day* in 2000, he attacked Higgins for using dialogue to replace action, narrative, and a coherent pattern.[1] His broadside invites a question with a long history, viz., can dialogue carry a novel? In his preface to *Joseph Andrews*, Henry Fielding, author of some forty plays, distinguished the aesthetic situation of the novel from that of stage drama by calling the novel a comic epic in prose. His distinction matters today. Whereas a play (or a movie) is seen with others in a

87

theater over a two-hour stretch, the novel makes different demands. The reader doesn't join others for a brief shared experience. Because, like the epic, the novel is something to be read, the novel reader is usually alone, and the time he spends reading, indeterminate. This last point is crucial. Not only do we read at different rates of speed; the same reader needs as much time to manage a page of William Faulkner as it takes him to sail through twenty of Agatha Christie.

Henry James (in *The Awkward Age*), Ivy Compton Burnett, and Henry Green all ignored Fielding's distinction. The ratio of speech to narration runs high in Higgins, too. That's how he planned it. "The quotes make the story. . . . Dialogue is character and character is plot," he insisted.[2] He doth protest too much. First of all, he's disregarding the weight of the unspoken and the repressed, Freudian themes developed by Beckett, Pinter, and even by Higgins himself (e.g., BL 11). As in D.H. Lawrence, practice can belie polemic in Higgins. But not to fret. The clash usually improves his art. He believes, for instance, that putting us inside his people's heads will win them, if not our sympathy, at least our enlightened understanding. But before doing this vital work, he has to know the people and their world cold.

Nor does he probe just anybody's psyche. Like James, he's highly selective in his choice of both person and moment. Also Jamesian is his urge ("Dramatize! Only dramatize!" James insisted) to write novels as lean, wiry, and tightly built as plays. Higgins's flair for self-withdrawal could beget a present-tense action as palpable as that occupied by the reader. The first sentence of *The Friends of Eddie Coyle*, "Jackie Brown at twenty-six, with no expression on his face, said that he could get some guns" (3), describes with matchless economy a person, a code, and a milieu. Without warning, the reader has been dropped inside a hyperactive field all the more menacing for its quietness. Peter Lewis might have had this swift, savage lyricism in mind when he said, "Reading a Higgins novel is like facing a firing squad armed with high-velocity rifles" (640).

Lewis's statement can't be read as unconditional praise. Even Higgins couldn't sustain the blend of shading and starkness found in the fist sentence of *Eddie Coyle*. He wouldn't have wanted to. A novel needs a mediating authorial voice lest its tightly framed scenes stretch out in a blinding glare. And even though novelistic self-erasure endows characters with freedom, it need not abandon them. Indirection helps Higgins lace his action with vital information while also making it clear that he's not a one-note writer. Like any other novelist, he has the right to exist. And he knows it. Except for its last page and a half, Chapter Sixteen of *Judgment*, which extends to thirteen pages, consists wholly of narration. The eight pages that go by in Chapter One of *A Year or so with Edgar* before a character speaks build credibility for both Higgins and his book. The thirteen pages of narration that open Chapter Six of *Kennedy for the Defense* put him beyond the pale of the dogmatically "pure" novel of Flaubert and his apostles, as well.

The inspiration and craft infusing such narrative passages can also attain a high level of artistry. Third-person commentary isn't a chore that Higgins wants to drop quickly so he can move on to what really interests him—reporting gossip. He'll extend his narrative passages to portray characters from both inside and out-, and thus orchestrate their confusions and tensions vis-à-vis those of others. The accuracy of these passages denotes respect—for both subject matter and reader, who deserves to be put in the picture. Dialogue without the companionability of narrative copies the jaggedness of existence, disallowing coherence—all in favor of the dubious goal of chopping life to a pattern of fitful episodes.

It also blurs the important division between theater and fiction. A mediating narrative voice preserves this edge, blocking the theft of a work of fiction by its characters. Books like those of Higgins need a narrating voice distinct from the experiencing voices of the people, i.e., gangsters whose lives keep growing more frantic. Higgins's careful, accurate voice both abets coherence and provides a leavening of sanity without competing with the spoken passages. It also gathers and stabilizes the lines of speech into a novelistic unit. We're grateful. Knowing that the novel we're reading isn't about to be high-jacked gives us the assurance to read intelligently. Narration in Higgins forms part of the fabric of a novel without overtaking the novel. It shows that a civilized moderating mind will both keep the novel from lurching into nonsense or exploding into blasts of gunfire. Ivan Sandoff's review of *Eddie Coyle* defines the challenge Higgins would keep setting himself: "The hoods are here—in your living room. The snout of the pistol is up your nose."[3] Sandoff has invited a big question: how can we breathe, let alone read, with the muzzle of a pistol pushing into our sinuses? Higgins holds our attention because we daren't look away.

I

He tried, in later works like *Agent* (1999) and *End of Day* (2000) to restore some of the vital signs that attracted so many readers to his first three books. This attempt put him at odds with his creative instincts. No artist likes to backtrack or chase his shadow, particularly one as determined as Higgins to keep testing himself anew. But the lukewarm public response to works like *Mandeville* (CADS 2, 10) made him rethink the merits of the shorter, leaner, harder-hitting books of his early publishing career. This is not to say that he scrapped all he had learned about his art between 1972 and the early 1990s. The author of *Mandeville* (1991) also wrote *Eddie Coyle*, and his middle and later books include effects absent from the earlier ones. Trying to compare works belonging to the two camps find us walking crabwise through a spectrum.

First, the drive toward narrative self-effacement ruled Higgins's fictional technique throughout his whole career. *A Change of Gravity* (1997) is as free of interpretation and analysis as his first three books; neither does this late work tell us *what* to think any more than it discloses what Higgins is thinking or feeling. But if dialogue—the vehicle through which characters convey their reality—is Higgins's main artistic gift, it's sometimes misjudged, as when Higgins asks it to do too much. For instance, the big dramatic moments in his work starting in the late 1980s, rather than breaking on the page, come to us warmed over—as topics of discussion hours after their occurrence. The people spend too much time reviewing what happened rather than inciting action of their own.

Also distracting and off-putting is the problem we sometimes have of keeping characters straight in our minds. All too often, Higgins's people bid for our attention without showing their faces or letting their voices be heard. Chapter Five of *Edgar*, for instance, extends an anecdote (89-97) about someone we never meet. Being expected to commit ourselves imaginatively to a no-show puts us off. Higgins didn't learn from this miscue, repeating it in Chapter Seven of *Wonderful Years*. Gary Dretzka found his next novel, *Trust*, marred by this weakening of grip: "the capers in the book," said Dretzka in the Chicago *Tribune*, "get awfully difficult to follow in spots, especially when it comes to recalling who owes what to whom and why."[4]

An explanation for such lapses lies in that pioneering study of fictional technique, Ford Madox Ford's *Joseph Conrad: A Personal Remembrance* (1924). Having co-written *The Inheritors* (1901) and *Romance* (1903), Ford and Conrad were working on a novel called *The Nature of A Crime* when Conrad died. Their collaboration sharpened their understanding of writing dialogue or directly reported speech. And most of Ford's recollections on the subject stem from his agreement with Conrad that dialogue plagued them more than any other aspect of their art. Like Higgins, these two impressionists believed in authorial self-naughting. But they looked more closely than Higgins did at the dangers of letting the characters' words steer the action. Pace, they saw, would flag. Ford reasoned, "directly reported speeches in a book . . . move very slowly," bilking the author of his chance to summarize, foreshadow, and provide transitions. He then ascribes the success of Conrad's *The Secret Agent* (1907) to this logic: "In [*Secret Agent*] there will be found . . . hardly any direct speech at all, and probably none that is more than a couple of lines in length."[5]

Ford might have framed this edict with Higgins in mind. Edgar Lannin, title figure of *A Year or So with Edgar*, spends much of his time alone, during which, presumably, he suffers from a build-up of verbal pressure. Anyone who joins him will soon suffocate under an avalanche of talk. Edgar's logorrhea erupts often, too, his long-windedness filling up all of Chapter Three of *Year or So* barring a few sentences. Yakking mars Higgins's better novels, too. Chapter Seven of *Impostors* recounts the trials of running a city saloon at a profit during the summer months. Cash-flow problems might have been vexing Higgins during the book's composition, Erwin Ford having pointed out that, in the late 1980s, he owed the IRS $400,000 (198). Perhaps Higgins found it therapeutic to rehearse the woes of food-and-drink peddlers. But he forgot that a novel isn't a therapy session. Relying on direct speech, Chapter Twenty-Six of *Impostors* says more than we need to know about the trials of serving and cleaning up after customers in a roadside bar-and-grill. *Bomber's Law* re-inscribes, again to

Higgins's detriment, the question of how heavy a load direct speech can carry in a work of fiction. In Lt. Brian Dennison and Harry Dell'Appa's wife Gayle, *Bomber* has two raisonneurs. i.e., choric figures who, rather than provoking action, comment on it.

The slowness with which their insights develop points another truth; Higgins is more of a monologist than a creator of the give-and-take of conversation, like that found in Elmore Leonard. Robert B. Parker made this point in 2004 (*Easiest* vii), building on Peter Lewis's words about "uninterrupted monologue" in Higgins: " Once his more articulate characters get into rhetorical stride," said Lewis, "the only thing that stops them is the end of a chapter" (640). And most of them *are* articulate. Although they may linger in the wings, once they move center stage, they'll speak so doggedly that, as Lewis claims, only a chapter break *can* silence them.

The verbal relentlessness of the archetypal Higgins figure often violates a key tenet of the art of writing for the human voice:

> To pretend [said Ford in 1924] that any character or any author writing directly can remember whole speeches with all their words for a matter of twenty-four hours, let alone twenty-four years, is absurd. The most that the normal person carries away of a conversation after even a couple of hours is just a . . . phrase or two, and the mannerism of the speaker. (198)

Ford is right. Higgins breaks faith with the reader when an ex-employee of the Defense Department in *Mandeville* recites verbatim a tirade directed to her twenty years earlier (91-2). The reader's distrust mounts. Later in the book, a non-native speaker of English quotes verbatim about 300 words of an English-language speech *he* heard twenty years before (179-80). Higgins tempers this implausibility by writing about characters as verbally skilled as good novelists: "My idea of slaw [says a man in Chapter Thirty-Eight of *Impostors*] is the runny stuff you get at the cheaper beachfront restaurants where they give you the fried clams and the scallops in cardboard boats, the french fries heaped up on paper plates, and the slaw in the big pleated paper cups" (296). But he has already lost too much artistic ground. A passage in *Judgment*, published ten years before *Impostors*, shows Deke not only repeating with perfect recall words said to him in conversation weeks earlier (50-1); he also gives in a passage of some 150 words an exact oral transcript of what his interlocutor claims *he* heard from a third party (33-4). This annoyance is standard practice in Higgins; in *Edgar*, a man spends sixteen pages quoting word-for-word, with only a few brief interruptions, a conversation he heard a year before (138-54).

What he says grates because it's unnatural. As Ford showed in *The Good Soldier* (1915), people summarize what they hear in conversation. Though we may single out the odd colorful phrase, we forget most of what we hear—if we're paying attention at all. Much of the time our minds wander, or we've tuned out in favor of working on a witty comeback. Higgins's disregard of this dynamic fuels novelistic mayhem. People quote people quoting other people, flyspecking the pages of his books with inverted commas while also burying us inside a Chinese box of words. Four out of five paragraphs in *Swan Boats* begin thus: " ' ' " (138); paragraphs end this way in *Penance* (106, 152), *Impostors* (325), and *Billy Ryan* (132).

The stylistic austerity imposed by Higgins's policy of self-effacement now reeks of self-indulgence. Better judgment might have precluded this botch; no novelist can manage so many plot lines by means of embedded dialogue as he tries to do. Ironically, the creations of this self-effaced author now sink under the weight of authorial intent. A good example of a Higgins novel that suffers from authorial overstepping is *Swan Boats* (1995). The book's first-rate subject, the sexual and emotional demands of adult relationships, pales inside scenes that stretch to agonizing length. The leaching starts immediately, *Swan Boats* beginning with pages and pages of somebody's precise recitation of somebody else's words. The issue—a complicated financial deal—will scare away most of the dazed survivors of this stretch of self-embedded dialogue. Which Higgins himself will distrust; to regain reader confidence, he treats Burton Rutledge's long reminiscence in Chapter Sixteen (180-92) as narrative, omitting inverted commas at the head of each paragraph, rather than as direct speech.

Ironically, the same acuity we admired in the earlier books we now fault as an obstacle to narrative flow. It gets worse. Besides holding us hostage to his adaptation of impressionistic technique, Higgins can overdo his attentiveness to detail. The richness of his verbal imagination outruns his sense of balance and proportion in *Mandeville Talent*, where his fussy rehearsal of the background of a murder case includes data that couldn't possibly help the police nail the culprit. This blunder is mitigated—but only just. Once a suspect comes to trial, the fog lifts, even though this development occurs to the side of the main action. Moving litigation to center stage clears the air still more. Higgins's eye for telling, evocative detail and his trial lawyer's familiarity with courtroom protocol engross readers of *Judgment, Change of Gravity*, and some of the Jerry Kennedy books as much as the trials being heard.

But these passages are too few. The later books, with their ripe descriptions of high-end luxury items and brand names, bog down in details of different kinds. Chapter Eleven of *Mandeville Talent*, for instance, spends too much time back-grounding the New York law firm that Joe Corey quit to investigate the murder, decades earlier, of his wife's grandfather in western Massachusetts. Higgins's interest in history grew with the years. Some of the historical data he shares with us can be a treat, like his on-the-wing remarks about the Chickering upright piano a dancing teacher might have installed in her studio to "pound out tap-practice tunes" (CG 101). But not all readers will feel treated. Some might disclaim the two-page sketch of Lillian Condon's dance studio as a pointless distraction after learning that the studio shut its doors decades before the book's present-tense action.

A police inspector in *Outlaws* says, "True artist is the one who knows when to stop" (116). The precept must have impressed Higgins because he repeated it three years later in *On Writing* (173). Unfortunately, he had trouble following it.

Because he'll never use two examples when he can find ten, his outstanding powers of observation recoil on him. Narrative economy in Higgins in his middle and late books is usually foiled by rhetorical razzle-dazzle. His reluctance to leave anything out, while confirming a healthy flair for experience, keeps road-blocking his people. He can't send one of them into a bar or restaurant without describing the place in detail and rehearsing its history (e.g., V 117). The more expensive the place, the more dutifully reverent his description of it, as if he's showing the world that he belongs at Locke Ober's top table alongside the Cabots and the Lodges. The introduction of any old established WASP fixture into one of his books can send him back several generations to the fixture's origins. Chapter Fourteen of *Sandra Nichols* backstories the posh Strothers School in Andover, Massachusetts (site of Phillips Academy, one of the country's oldest prep schools), commenting fastidiously on the school's architecture, its founder, and her educational goals (159-66).

As Higgins's cars, boats, and wardrobe grew more costly, his prose style filled out. Yes, the dialogue still snaps and stings. Nor did moving his fictional setting from the tough inner city to the suburbs mar his ability to write passages of raffish immediacy. But he also drifts stylistically into long, dreamy sentences laden with sub-clauses. A Jamesian, sometimes Churchillian, intricacy of statement ousts the earlier, cleaner, more reader-friendly prose. Sentences can run half a page. The over-explicitness of the following paragraph, which opens Chapter Twenty-seven of *Outlaws*, engulfs the reader. Though Higgins's intentions in writing the paragraph may have been brave, his execution flagged (note that an active verb drives only one of the five sentences in the quoted passage). Raymond Chandler would never have written it; nor would the Higgins of *Eddie Coyle*:

> The store at the eastern end of the block on the north side of the Waterford Shopping Plaza was a big MediMart. Blue and white posters in its window advertised a coupon sale of mouthwashes, panty hose, sanitary napkins, shaving cream and motor oil. Next to it was a Dunkin' Donuts coffee shop. Two telephone company trucks, a blue and white Ford Bronco II carrying police shield logos on its doors, a white US Mail truck and two private cars were parked in front of the doughnut shop. There were small clusters of two and three cars . . . near the entrances to the First National Bank of Waterford, the Omnidentix Clinic and the Commonwealth Savings and Loan offices. (196)

The red flags were flying from the start. More than 60 words divide a sentence's noun subject from its main verb in *Edgar* (162). The later rhetoric can slacken more alarmingly. A sentence in *Bomber's Law* includes a parenthesis of some 100 words (22-3). Later in the book, we're blindsided by a self-embedded sentence so baroque in design that eleven lines of print divide a noun from the adjectival clause that modifies it (65). The qualifications and deferrals of Henry James's late prose alight upon a 300-word aside in *Sandra Nichols* (212-3). The first words of the sentence following the one warped by this long parenthesis, "But I digress, as usual" (213), shows that Higgins should have organized his materials better—and that he knew it.

Artistic decline shows elsewhere. Narrative texture and pace in the middle and later books aren't nearly as palpable as heretofore. At issue are Higgins's lapses in concentration. Whereas the early works hid the great effort poured into them, control in their later counterparts trails off. Dialogue and atmospherics, though as real as ever, wheeze inside the books' drowsy pace. Starting with *Judgment* (1976), many of the works, like *Choice, Victories, Swan Boats*, and *Sandra Nichols*, meander in a maze of subplots. Higgins's statement that he wrote fast "to find out how the story came out" (CADS 1, 31), infers a misplaced faith in the creative unconscious. Rather than taking charge of a scene, he'll hang around and see how it unfolds. His adoptive role of passive recorder has made him vulnerable to distraction. Paragraphs and even chapters waver in focus, dwelling too long on side issues. Though dramatic on their own, these by-ways, like a dinner-table argument about wine in *Bomber's Law* (262), both stall the action and neglect the people. Structural damage occurs, too. Whereas Sgt. Bob Brennan shows his face often in the first half of *Judgment*, his physical absence in most of the book's second half limits him to providing fodder for discussion.

The Dell'Appas' marriage in *Bomber* calls up another problem that bedeviled Higgins from the start—extracting brisk, sophisticated comedy out of conversations between married couples. In *Kennedy for the Defense* (1980), the first Jerry Kennedy book, he modeled the talk of Jerry and his wife Joan, or Mack, on the witty, nuanced dialogue of Nick and Nora Charles in Hammett's *The Thin Man* (1934). The scenes featuring Jerry and Mack missed the mark. Higgins tried a different approach in *Bomber*. But the book's arch, self-conscious pseudo-chic repartee, which also appears in *Patriot Game, Choice*, and *Gravity*, stumbles, too. The first time Harry and Gayle Dell'Appa appear on the page together, in Chapter Two, Harry alludes to Cole Porter and *Beowulf*, and Gayle quotes *Hamlet* (20). Names keep dropping. Later in the chapter, after mentioning Agatha Christie's Miss Jane Marple, Gayle calls him Natty Bumppo (38). We're flummoxed. Wouldn't a couple have depleted its store of literary references after ten years of marriage? Higgins provokes a similar question in *Mandeville Talent* when Joe and Jill Corey quote at least one Shakespearean play in four of their conversations (61, 103, 122, 148), a quirk that makes us ask if Higgins's very subject matter was too white for 1991.

Or if Higgins could write plausible dialogue between two educated people who aren't discussing the law or concocting a scheme. The people needn't be lovers or spouses. Harry Dell'Appa's chats with the book's other choric figure, Lt. Brian Dennison, are stuffed with allusions; the dialogue between the two men in Chapter Seven cites Shakespeare's *Lear*, Dickens's *Bleak House*, Andrew Marvell, and T.S. Eliot (BL 114, 106, 116, 121). Poor judgment on Higgins's part also mangles the final chapter. The punctuation ending a paragraph there, " ' ' " (268), implies that all of the players in the scene we've been reading have total recall of all their prior conversations stretching back several months. Why invite this implication instead of doing the more sensible work of framing the novel's finale? Another mind-scrambling sentence in the chapter names seven characters, only one of whom has appeared live (269-70).

Another stylistic gaffe that mars Higgins's late work carries forward from his novelistic debut. The opening sentence of Chapter Nine of *Eddie Coyle* (1972) reads, "Jackie Brown found the Microbus *on* the upper level *of* the Undercommon Garage *near* the stairs *to* the kiosk *at* Beacon and Charles Streets" (60), emphasis added). The right-branching sentence that grows by piling up prepositional phrases also opens the first chapter of *Trust* (1989) (1). Its recurrence at the tops of Chapters Six (55) and Seventeen (289) causes special regret. These examples of lazy writing turn up in places where they're most likely to be noticed and thus leave a more lasting stink. Higgins sometimes needs a sharper editor. The same sentence in *Penance* uses the verb, looked, to convey different meanings (228); *Penance* also shows him putting meaning into an adverb rather than the ill-chosen verb it modifies (291). Careful proofreading, finally, could have also condensed the phrase, "an exceptionally talented person," from *Impostors* (299), to one word.

II

Higgins's flaws and oversights need to be judged fairly. Some of them rise from his failure to temper his genius with talent. Capable of writing twenty to forty pages a day, and on some days even a hundred (Doyle 24), he put most of his effort into urging his books forward. Most of his editing skills he directed to the work submitted by his creative writing students. But this is an explanation, not an excuse. Mistakes of different kinds foul his art, and they must factor into any assessment of it. What they disclose, finally, is that there's much more in Higgins to admire than to scathe.

Time and again, he'll stagger us with both the level and detail of his insights, some of which come from diligent preparation; only when the mind has done its work will the creative instincts fire up. A good deal of research and thought stoked his vivid, graceful books. His creative use of some of it makes him look prophetic. The statement of a journalist in *Dreamland* (1977), for instance, "You might well wonder . . . what the hell a Bahamian corporation executive would want with a West Virginia paint company" (97), forecasts the advent of corporate diversification in the 1980s along with problems caused by migrant workers in our new century. Solid preparation also boosts Higgins's treatment of his materials. Chapter Fifteen of *Patriot Game*, for example, rolls to a strong dramatic climax. But Higgins opens Chapter Sixteen miles away with a new set of characters. This is no lapse. Higgins has deployed the art of inter-cutting to fold in ideas and information that will lend force to the issues he had brought to a head at the end of the previous chapter.

Mercifully, no big ideas intrude; Higgins understands that intellectualism in a work of fiction can shrink and shrivel whatever it touches. Sure of its worth, his best fiction spurns polemic, too. Higgins knows his turf. Unlike some of his fellow writers, whose books are cheap and sensational or dry and indigestible, he usually opts for a sequence of dramatic scenes that unfold smoothly. Wisely, he ruled out structural convolutions from the start. By sticking to accessibility, plainness, and readability, he dispelled the myth that important fiction has to be cerebral. He proved, too, that complex, intense matters *can* be dealt with simply without being trivialized. This common sense tallies with his intelligent sympathy for his subjects. He writes as if he knows his characters personally, and his descriptions are both lyrical and precise with few hints of weakness or flagging inspiration queering the pitch.

Higgins reinvented crime fiction to suit both himself and his city on the Charles. Even if you can't summarize one of his books after finishing it, you'll have had a gripping read. What's more, you won't know what to expect the next time. Max Boot noted in the *Christian Science Monitor* in 1992 that Higgins tests himself anew in each book, "trying to push the envelope."[6] This artistic daring merits acclaim. Higgins has the artistic self-confidence to flee success. Though he sometimes slips up, he also rejects familiar novelistic turf to mine the edge of his inventive powers. Like John le Carré, he keeps moving and staying up to date. Le Carré shifted smoothly from Cold War espionage to topics like the dirty tricks played by drug cartels in *The Constant Gardener* (2000), and Higgins's eye turned, though not completely, from street crime to foul play in executive board rooms, the courts, and high-stake local politics.

His practice of writing about lawbreakers puts his books in the dovecote of crime fiction, even though they subjugate criminal acts to the effects the acts have on those touched by them; in *Mandeville Talent*, the circuit takes twenty years to form. The shocks and surprises Higgins delivers can't be predicted. He has taken crime fiction beyond entertainment and moral instruction. Perhaps his rivetingly readable work is challenging rather than cozy because it extends the category of crime fiction, a category or genre more important to his readers than to him given his belief that people are sinners by nature. Call it what you like; if this is formula writing, the formula still works.

It worked for Robert Manning, editor of *Atlantic*, who ranked Higgins alongside Bellow and Updike, claiming, "I think his work is absolutely, totally unique, and will be read and reread by many subsequent generations. That, my friend, is literature" (Doyle 24). But classic literary fiction has also been called work that everybody praises but nobody reads. Higgins, alas, occupies this dusty niche. The vast majority of his books are both out of print and likely to remain so. The title of Frank L. Kaplan's 2004 review of *Easiest Thing*, "Not for the Casual Reader of Crime Fiction,"[7] grazes Higgins's fierce individualism. Higgins writes his books in his own way, and that's that. They don't ask to be liked. They don't have to. Their author has joined a rare and unusual vision to a firm narrative stance—a good enough reason to win our attention and even our admiration most of the time.

Notes

1. Bruce Desilva, "Get out of Jail Free," New York *Times Book Review*, 20 August 2000, 15.

2. "USC News—Boston Writer's Archive finds new home at the University of South Carolina"*http://uscnews.sc.edu/libr045.html*, 3 May 2004, 2.

3. Ivan Sandrof, "Better than 'Godfather,'" Worcester *Sunday Telegraph*, 12 March 1972, 86.

4. Gary Dretzka, "Trust George Higgins to weave a winner," Chicago *Tribune*, 14: 5.

5. Ford Madox Ford, *Joseph Conrad: A Personal Remembrance* (1924; New York: Octagon, 1971), 199-200.

6. Max Boot, "Police-Beat Writer Spins City Tales," *Christian Science Monitor*, 22 September 1992, 12.

7. Frank L. Kaplan, "Not for the Casual Reader of Crime Novels," *Rocky Mountain* [Denver] *News*, 5 November 2004, 27(D).

Chapter Seven

With Friends Like These

Though sparsely documented, the exploits of small-time hoods can be as colorful as those of their chiefs. Eddie Coyle's life stinks, and, bad as it is, it's slipping away from him. He lives near the rank bottom of Boston's underworld food chain, a bad place to be if things go wrong, as they're bound to do for hard-luck Eddie. Nothing in his life is safe. Careful narrative selection shows, first, the lack of balance and warmth in this ex-con's home. He refers to his wife casually in Chapter Eighteen of the thirty-chapter *Friends of Eddie Coyle*, and, when she does show her face, in Chapter Twenty-Five, it's only for half a page or so (157), during which she calls him a stranger in his own home.

This eponym of *Friends* is acting out a version of Scott Fitzgerald's belief that American lives have no second acts. Lacking the tough ruthlessness of Jerry "Digger" Doherty and Jackie Cogan, the title figures of Higgins's next two books, Coyle resembles a Cornell Woolrich anti-hero with the crushing sense of loneliness and fear that keeps building in him. Higgins spelled out his problem: "He is too old to do any more time and the only way he could avoid doing time for a crime he committed is by turning snitch" (CADS 2, 3). Here's the background of the dilemma Higgins is talking about. Some weeks before the book's present-tense action, Coyle was convicted of the federal crime of trucking 200 cases of stolen Canadian Club whisky across state lines into New Hampshire. At forty-five or so, this fleshy, feverish ex-con doubts if he could survive another jail term. And besides being too old for the rigors of the joint, he also wants to spare his youngsters the jeers of their schoolmates.

Higgins pulls us into the grungy heart of his darkness by capturing him during that interim between his conviction and his sentencing. Coyle is looking to bargain. His bringing about a major arrest might convince the authorities that he has reformed, and they, in turn, he hopes, might recommend a reduced or suspended sentence. He struggles to win the authorities' favor, his controller at the U.S. Treasury saying of him, "he gets around more'n any man I ever seen" (84).

After a great deal of soul-wringing, he snitches on Jackie Brown, the arms dealer who sold him a cache of weapons in Chapter One, setting up the arrest of Jackie at the very spot Jackie had picked to deliver five M-Sixteen machine guns to another buyer. This action, Coyle believes, warrants him a recommendation of leniency. He's wrong. The lawmen who could lighten his sentence in New Hampshire occupy a different zone of authority from the ones Coyle delivered Jackie to in Massachusetts. What's more, they know it. The snitching of Jackie falls short of the "strong reason" (9) needed to convince the New Hampshire court of Coyle's rehabilitation, even though Jackie's arrest with a trunk full of unregistered machine guns could jail him for life. Though valuable, Coyle's help in the Jackie Brown grab is merely "a start" (130), according to Dave Foley, a federal cop and his Treasury office contact. The cops in New Hampshire want to nab the masterminds of the Canadian Club heist that caused Coyle's troubles to begin with.

A quick study, Coyle sees that he lacks bargaining chips. And what this means for him is that his survival demands his becoming "stoolie permanent' (133), i.e., an informer who's always on call. No wonder he's agonizing. He's fungible. The agents he has been helping don't care about him. "Ah well . . . tough shit" (168), a T-man responds to Dave Foley's remark that Coyle has nothing to bargain with. Harried and badgered, the man called Eddie Fingers (e.g., 69, 145) busies himself in different parts of town scrabbling with ever diminishing luck at ways to stay free. He can't afford to relax. Despite having had his fingers in so many different pies, he'll die from a surfeit of beer.

So drunk does he get at a Boston Bruins hockey game that, asleep in the front seat of a car supposedly taking him to a party, he's a sitting duck (he's called "The Duck" [73]) for the slugs fired into his head from the back seat. The slugs should have been fired elsewhere, if at all. Ironically, after a lifetime in crime, Coyle dies for a wrong he never committed. In Chapter Twenty-Two, air hostess Wanda Emmett tells a state trooper-friend she sees at Logan Airport about some weapons delivered to the trailer she was sharing with her gangster boyfriend, Jimmy Scalisi. Jimmy Scal didn't only organize the three bank robberies recounted in the book; he also insulted Wanda and then beat her up. Her revenge is perfect. Scalisi is one of the four thieves ambushed by the police in Chapter Twenty-Four at the home of the banker whose help they were counting on while holding his wife hostage.

Thus Coyle pays for Wanda's treachery, a twofold act of justice that chimes with his retributive code of ethics. Wanda betrayed Scalisi because she deserved better from a live-in married lover whose spoils she had been banking during her free time in Florida and Nassau. This notorious thief, part-time hired gun, and woman beater had to be stopped. Coyle's punishment, though harsher, is also just. Don't call him collateral damage. He had chosen to work in a dangerous environment where nobody can be trusted. Lacking options and running out of time, he relieved pressure by getting drunk. Though betrayed by his assassin, the bartender Dillon—who ironically is also his confidant—Coyle had been undermining himself for decades as a professional crook. The sins that Higgins's fellow Irish-American had piled up merit punishment, both in their own right and for smirching a proud heritage that will shape Higgins's sense of justice in later novels.

But Higgins didn't build a first-rate novel around Eddie Coyle simply to crush him. A novel driven by such pinchbeck justice wouldn't excel the way *Friends* does. Though a bottom feeder, Coyle also fuses features of Higgins's knowledge of Boston, a criminal justice system that swathes the FBI, the U.S. Treasury, the Massachusetts State Police, and an underworld Higgins had been studying since becoming a criminal lawyer in 1967. His thoughtful, nuanced view of that underworld transcends textbook morality. It includes the truth that Coyle has put himself beyond punishment in the familiar sense. His career as a gangster includes so much deprivation, loss, and pain that it has already undone him and, by extension, his hapless family. No wonder his wife and kids aren't named; Coyle's rogue life has reduced them to ciphers. His midlife death, no shock, carries forward from an ongoing death drift. Exempted from judging him, Higgins can make revelations about him that come only from giving him and his circle his full attention.

I

We're convinced early that Coyle deserves this care. Called "a small timer" (87) by Foley and "a little fish" (149) by Dillon, he could never excel in any line of work, crooked or honest. But he *has* cultivated good street sense and other survival skills. Though his outlook had dimmed at the time of his death, he dies from a communication mishap; Wanda Emmett, not he, divulged the information that rolled up the Scalisi gang. Coyle had no way to protect himself, which he might have otherwise done; two characters, a lawman and a fellow thug, agree that he's "not stupid" (151). They're right. Known as "the stocky man" (e.g., 4), the Duck, and Eddie Fingers as well as by his own name, he assumes different identities as protective coloring. And, though pudgy, out of shape, and old for his desperate line of work, he acts decisively when action is called for. The federal cop Dave Foley, who was already impressed by his busyness, notes of him in Chapter Fourteen, "this guy's all over the place all of a sudden" (83). But Foley also called him "a creature of habit" (28).

It's fitting that this lowlife is the subject of so much talk in the 1972 book that bears his name. Though aware of the benefits of action, he also knows that any lucky break he catches could dissolve in acts of rashness and improvidence if he let them. Not only must he give wide berth to the police; his fellow crooks can hurt him more than the law. And, as a small-timer, he's a more likely target for trouble than the bigger fry, which means practically all his collaborators. He keeps breaking the law after his conviction in New Hampshire because crime is the only life he knows. Higgins writes about this nobody because, like so many of us, he's struggling to survive the best way he can and—even during the good times—barely scraping by.

His instinct for survival comes into play immediately. Negotiating the price of contraband weapons in Chapter One, he holds his poise, telling his trading partner, "We got to talk some more about price, I see that" (7), rather than flying into a rage or sinking to sarcasm. He lies and is lied to in turn by Jackie Brown in this scene, as is common in the illicit gun trade. But Coyle pierces the fog of falsehoods by arguing that his buying in bulk (thirty side arms) entitles him to a lower price than the one Jackie has been quoting. Coyle's sales technique stays strong. In Chapter Three, now in the role of seller, he tells a bank robber who needs some guns that he can get him some Smith and Wessons, a Colt Python, and two Rugers with "big ventilated ribs" (21).

Higgins has joined Coyle to his bourgeois readers. Any number of salesmen in textbooks, clothing, or tires could learn from him. Like all good sales reps, Coyle encourages people to trade with him. He wins the bank robber's trust with his knowledge of both the availability and the advantages of certain products in his inventory over others (of the Ruger, he says reassuringly, "you could hold up a bank all by yourself with that thing" [21]). The inclusion in his store of support items, in this case, shells, wins him his client's confidence and clinches him the sale.

But that client robs banks, which explains why Coyle hasn't brought his store of weapons and shells with him. A bank robber would sooner steal contraband rather than pay for it. And Coyle's business associates are *all* thugs. He differs from most salesmen in the hurdles he must leap to net a profit. The high-risk business he's in tests his survival instincts along with his salesmanship. Thus he utters early in the first chapter of *Friends* the foundation creed of his trade: "I get paid for being careful" (5). When told by his bank robber-client in Chapter Three, "I heard something about Dillon I didn't like," his answer, "I heard that too" (18), conveys, besides a willingness to take what's offered him, his well-judged reluctance to probe subjects knowledge of which might hurt him.

He had already shown his mettle. His first words to Jackie in Chapter One, "I don't know as I like buying stuff from the same lot as somebody else" (3), voice a fear that belies his casual tone. He's loath to buy guns from a job lot that has supplied other hoods. As he says, one of these hoods might use his gun to commit murder, and the gun could be traced to the lot that provisioned Coyle, who could then be arrested both as an accessory and for dealing weapons without a permit. This danger persists because some thugs—being thugs—flout a basic law of the underworld. They hang on to their unfired guns after a job, despite knowing that a pristine weapon can be traced as easily as one that has been fired.

Coyle has already paid dearly for ignoring the truth that gangs are combat-ready para-military units that exact harsh punishment for all infractions. The law traced a weapon Coyle had bought from a broken lot, and because the gangster it was traced to went to jail, Coyle had to pay for brokering the deal (just as Jackie Brown had to tell Coyle straightaway that the guns he's offering come from broken lots). The convicted gangster's pals shut Coyle's left hand in a drawer and kicked the door shut. Coyle got the name Eddie Fingers because of the extra set of knuckles this act of rough justice gave him. The broken bones in his hand may even be a bizarre gift. The same joints that ache in bad weather and that can't bend in any weather remind him of the penalties of crossing the mob. Why complain? He has accepted his punishment in the same spirit in which it was inflicted—as a normal condition of his job. His punishers weren't angry with him. Coyle had sold a gun with a history and had to pay for his mistake. The "friends" (4) of the convicted gangster operate from laws that override friendship. Their policy of punishing those who make mistakes that go against their interests, they and Coyle know, means good business.

The retribution that dogs Coyle grows in cruelty. Higgins says of his killer, "Dillon is a psychopath and certainly wouldn't consider himself to be a criminal. He's merely doing things that have to be done" (Brady 25). Has Higgins misjudged him? Dillon is more than a technician who does jobs he has drained of moral content. This convicted felon who tends a bar frequented by crooks takes $20 a week from Dave Foley for reporting what he hears them say; he also works as a gang enforcer. This regimen is breaking him down. He enters the novel in Chapter Six thus: "Dillon explained that he was frightened" (33). He says immediately that he needs protection "while hunched over to protect his stomach" (33), which, he claims, has soured from all the coffee he drinks (he may have cancer). He's also suffering from insomnia, which could come from his being parted from his wife, or ex-wife (57).

Perhaps his insomnia stems from adultery. The banker Robert L. Biggers of suburban Duxbury, who's having an affaire with a younger colleague, always a portent in Higgins, has insomnia, too (123). And he dies in the same chapter in which he's introduced. The slugs that pierce his body in the presence of his popsy have the force of retribution. And even though Nancy Williams, fresh out of high school, is unmarried, the image of her married lover slumping to his death will foul *her* digestion and cost *her* hours of sleep (like Dillon and Biggers) in the decades to come. She suffers for a reason. Infidelity is a crime, and criminals to the conservative-minded Higgins must forfeit normal human joys. Like his counterpart Dillon, the hit man Jackie Cogan will also have trouble sleeping (CT 148). Dillon won't or can't drink.

In an offbeat way, his abstinence helps him tend bar effectively. Without being asked, he pours a harried Coyle a double whisky and a beer within a day of accepting a contract to kill him. Guilt has urged him to lavish drinks on his mark; he also praises Coyle's moral courage in having gone to jail for a crime committed by a senior thug. Without knowing it, Coyle has touched a small, soft place inside Dillon. The same Dillon that's going to kill him befriends Eddie Coyle during the last hours of his life.

Jackie Brown also displays gentleness after clinching his arms deal with Coyle at the very end of Chapter One (9). The smile he flashes challenges the truth that criminals must sink their hearts. Jackie is smiling at the man who'll later rat on him, and, were Coyle calmer when he walked into Dillon's bar in Chapter Twenty Eight, he'd have noticed that the kindness being heaped on him belies Dillon's customary impassiveness. But Jackie is either brighter than Dillon or, as a gun dealer rather than a hired gun, less weakened by the inhumanity of his job. Higgins begins three chapters of *Friends*, including the first and the last, by introducing him "with no expression on his face" (3, 115, 180).

This master of the stony look may have no fictional forebears. He occupies a different galaxy from the archetypal hero in Kafka, a young man who's arrested for a mysterious crime he can't remember committing. Though Jackie shares the deadpan indifference along with the last name of Graham Greene's Pinkie Brown in *Brighton Rock* (1938), he has holds no truck with the malice and cruelty that mark Pinkie's dirty deeds. In fact, survival to Jackie means casting off all the mystery and poetry he had ever learned, demented or otherwise. *Friends* isn't a coming-of-age story. Rather than breaking free at the end to a wider, freer world, Jackie is hobbled by having seen too much too soon. He knows all he needs to know about himself. This twenty-six-year-old whose words open the novel is a cold, empty vessel without a past, a nihilist whose reality is conveyed by the sale of arms.

In place of an interior life, Higgins has given him a functioning kind of insight, good judgment, and an instinct for self-preservation. Like Coyle, he has an impressive knowledge of his wares, their availability, assembly, and components; he'll even spell out the advantages of a Colt revolver with a two-inch barrel over a four-inch Smith and Wesson. And he gives nothing away. When asked if his supplier works in an armory, he says, "I got guns to sell" (7). He thrives on secrecy and innuendo. When approached by Coyle in Chapter One, he never asks Coyle's name. In fact, he'd rather *not* know it, in case his deal with Coyle goes wrong. He'll even hide his traces to protect himself. When he does refer to Coyle he gives his age as thirty-six or -seven (31), even though Coyle had just told him that he was rising forty-five (13).

Starting with a small, sharp scene, *Friends* isn't a happy story, but a gripping one. Never mind that the people are unsympathetic. Robert B. Parker explains how the smell of calamity brewing hits us straightaway: "We are in the story smack up against it . . . with no warning. . . . We are witnessing a story as it unfolds, almost narrationless, entirely dramatized" (Easiest, vii). Along with some of the book's other commentators, like William Vesterman (225), Parker also finds great merit in the book's opening sentence: "Jackie Brown at twenty-six, with no expression on his face, said that he could get some guns" (3). The menace *has* kicked in. This youngster with a heart of flint has made a flat, matter-of-fact statement that erases all doubt. The portent created by his implacable self-assurance energizes Higgins's ongoing practice of calling him by his full name. We're shaken. With daunting unselfconsciousness, Jackie Brown sells weapons that could be used to commit murder.

But even though his hardness fends off sympathy, he's more of a person than a predicament. The expressionless face he displays at the outset of the book's first and last chapters conveys his dead-end life. He has completed a circuit, which includes his twenty-seventh birthday. His lone sign of humanity, the smile he flashes at the end of Chapter One, is an anomaly he'd probably regret as a sign of weakness, if not a downright handicap to the effectiveness his loveless trade demands of him.

Like that of Coyle, Jackie's ongoing act of self-betrayal tallies with the rattlesnake narrative, an episode of descriptive amplitude embedded in a tightly wrapped story, featured in Chapter Seven. The thematic consequences of this contrast have been noted. William McPherson, reviewing *Friends* in, the *Washington Post*, called the life the novel depicts "banal, often dreary, and deadly as a rattlesnake."[1] Higgins's awareness of the snake's traditional association with poison, deceit, and treachery floods the canon. A cop tells a backstabbing colleague in *Bomber's Law* (1993), "If God makes you an offer to come back in your next life as a rattlesnake, you'll turn him down. . . . You'll say, 'No God . . .. I was one of those in my past life'" (287). This jibe sharpens the rattler's importance in *Friends*, the subject of which Higgins told the editor-in-chief of Little, Brown Publishers, was betrayal.[2]

The most radiant symbol of treachery, or betrayal, in the western world remains the snake. Banker Samuel Partridge knows this. While being held at gunpoint as he and his abductors are waiting for the time lock on the bank's vault to open, he thinks of the rattler that broke the calm of his family's lakeside vacation the previous summer. The anxiety it caused was brief. Though it frightened the Partridges, it didn't send them home. It had probably occupied the area for years without harming anyone, the family members agreed. Though the comparison is skewed, Sam has likened the team of bank robbers menacing him to the snake. They're local, they're dangerous, and they represent an evil that will never go away. But some caution and good sense—in the form of obeying their instructions—can quiet the evil and, for the nonce, draw its fangs.

Perhaps Sam's survival stems from his kinship to the snake. He recalls standing in the same patch of sunlight that warmed the snake, and he offers the snake a fish, just as he'll gladly surrender his bank's cash to the robbers. Does his complicity join him to that terrible aboriginal calamity Cardinal Newman saw engulfing humanity? The propitiatory fish reminds us that Coyle, whose name evokes the coil snakes often wrap themselves in, is called "a little fish" (149). We're being reminded that the fish symbolizes Christ. Coyle, who both betrays and *is* betrayed by his cronies, focuses the treachery in the book that bears his name. We think of him when Sam Partridge discourages the robbers from shooting out the bank cameras; the workers in the neighboring drug store would hear the shots and call the police (50). Yes, Sam is helping the robbers flee with the loot, but he's also preventing violence. The robbers are touched by his complicity, as the parting words of their spokesman to him show: "And thanks for your cooperation" (53).

Cooperative and deferential, Sam leaves the bank robbery with a taint on him. But thanks to his good judgment and fast thinking, no one touched by it, either at the bank or at home, where his family was being held at gunpoint, got hurt. He embraced the bad to prevent the worst, which is perhaps the most he can do in the corrupt world fashioned in large part by the Jesuit-schooled Higgins's reading of St. Augustine and Graham Greene. And don't forget James

Joyce. Sam Partridge, the hero of the theft incident, was given a bird's name in recognition of the divine import of his deeds. Though stained, these deeds also saved lives, a stroke of great moral value that evokes Joyce's equation of birds with things of the spirit in *A Portrait of the Artist as a Young Man*. Another religious echo: the whole bank robbery episode, from the abduction of the Partridges in their family room to the lurching movements of a dazed, blindfolded Sam after he's dropped off on a country road, takes place in Chapter Seven. The number, seven, combining four, which denotes the physical world (the points of the compass, the seasons, the humors, and the elements) and three, the world of spirit set forth by the Trinity, proclaims a totality in Christian iconography; it's God's number. The action of Chapter Seven embodies a microcosm of our post-lapsarian, that is, fallen world.

The snake that anchors the chapter plays the same vital role in Christian myth as his symbolic offspring and fellow avatar of betrayal, Judas. Higgins takes our fallen world on its own vile terms by using it as a vehicle for his artistic growth. The snake is described with great care. The rich auditory imagery of the sentence, "The snake turned slowly on the ground, its weight rubbing the pebbles against each other" (48), prefigures Higgins's description of a squad of bank robbers "walking in the grass at the edge of the crushed stone walk" (153) in Chapter Twenty Four. Not only is the leader of this squad Jimmy Scalisi, whose last name sounds like that of Judas Iscariot. The sensuous, nearly hypnotic quality of Higgins's description of the snake, contrasting with the swift, hard prose dominating the action to this point, also imparts a mythic power. Rejecting Sam Partridge's fish, the snake is the strongest living being in the book. And Higgins, by putting himself on a par with it in order to capture its reality, conveys the dread it has amassed over the past 2000 years.

Yes, the snake narrative infers a symbolic pattern that joins with, illuminates, and deepens the developing action. Appearing after six chapters of bright, agile prose, mostly in the form of dialogue, the resonant, highly charged episode creates a polyphony that serves two important ends: it shows that Higgins is not a one-note writer and that *Friends* is not a one-note book. Rather, it implicates us more deeply than we had heretofore realized in a universal tragedy. We have to read on. And we can't ask for much more than that.

II

Higgins's refusal to take his readers where they want to go has been thickening the brew. This triumph of artistic self-confidence, all the more remarkable for coming from a young writer, turns on the strategy of ignoring our comfort zones in favor of the off-key, the skewed, and the repellent. Regaling us with material that's snug, relaxing, and friendly would blunt our critical faculties. That's why *Friends* keeps readers of conventional or conservative crime fiction alert and sharp (why does Chapter Two begin with Coyle drinking a strawberry ice-cream soda [12]?). Though the book's three murders make death a force, *Friends* doesn't play on our fear of death. We don't identify with the banker whose death both occurs off the page and reaches us as a bald factual statement in a newspaper story. The other two murder victims, Coyle and the womanizing Bob Biggers, are both Judases the world can do without. What's more, Coyle's assassin doesn't get caught, so justice isn't served. The danger that this bilking of justice puts forth bucks the idea, often endorsed by Victorian fiction, in a larger moral, social, and cosmic order where the self is solid beyond all question and doubt.

By contrast, Higgins's outlook in *Friends* is the modern one of anxiety. Coyle has to connect his shaky sense of self to a society ruled by chance, betrayal, and a cruel code of laws that has already smashed his hand. How to pick his way through this urban minefield? Events as different as the sinking of the *Titanic* in 1912 and the destruction of the World Trade Center in 2001 have razed longstanding boundaries between order and chaos. But notably it's the lack of friendly, reliable guidelines that enables Higgins to describe, through Coyle, an experience both deeply familiar and more than a bit strange. Erwin H. Ford discussed this tricky blend in 1988: "The central problem of the book is not to solve a crime. The central problem is to choose a community against which to sin in order to remain in some [other] community. Eddie decides to sell information about Jackie Brown, the weapons dealer, to the police" (104).

The title of Higgins's 1984 novel, *A Choice of Enemies*, looms into view. Coyle must choose his enemies and pray for the best. His dilemma strikes home. Besides making decent people question their faith in human goodness, Higgins has fingered the strange and hidden in *us*. *Friends* offers a pathway into life, like all good fiction. But the road ends in a mirror meeting that makes us wince. Coyle and his friends peg into traits we dislike in ourselves. The point is made most often by dialogue. Contrast is the essence of drama, a key proposition to a writer as committed as Higgins to the scenic or dramatic method. Thus Chapter One of *Friends* describes a conversation between a buyer and a seller, one of whom is young and the other, middle aged.

But Higgins uses similarities as well as differences to develop *Friends*, and he uses them to greatest effect in places where they're not usually found. His disclosing common ground in what look like moral opposites, for instance, can chill the hearts of all churchgoing supporters of diligence, economy, and restraint. These foursquare values also rule the underworld. Higgins's analogy between the cheat and the churchgoer, though not exact, is close enough to merit a look. The anarchy normally linked to the underworld is bogus. A good crook, for whom violence is always regrettable, exercises the same caution, care, and control as the skilled business executive, surgeon, or banker. Their common respect for regularity and steadiness explains why Sam Partridge and his bank robber-captors work so smoothly. Arthur Valantropo, rather than cuffing Sam around. speaks gently and courteously to him, counseling prudence while calling him by name. He knows how to get things done.

The robbery succeeds because he has convinced Sam that that they share a common goal. "Just keep calm and be sensible," he advises Sam. "It isn't your money. It's all insured. We want the money. We don't want to hurt anybody. We will, but we don't want to" (44). This is the voice of reason, even though it's heard through a nylon mask. Valantropo is doing business in a peaceful, professional way. A second bank robbery, depicted in Chapter Twenty, fails because one of the robbers shoots a loan officer for signaling the police. Bob Biggers's killer should have avoided playing the avenger. Not only did his gunplay shorten the escape time of his team of thieves; it also ratcheted up the robbery to a capital case, which dictates a more thorough, concentrated police search conducted by more and better-trained searchers. Violence is always a mistake in Higgins. As Valantropo says, "killing somebody's the surest way to get a goddamned army after you" (152).

Mobsters like Artie Val respect the poise and deliberateness of other professional crooks even when these virtues go against their interests. When asked by a Mafia chief to murder Coyle that very night, Dillon refuses. He even holds his ground when threatened. A successful hit, he insists, requires time and preparation. Dillon, whose job as a barman has taught him the values of warmth and hospitality, also prides himself in his mettle as an enforcer. He won't do shoddy work. Nor will he leave matters to chance. Only the intended victim will be hurt, and his assassin will be both paid and allowed to manage his safe flight from the hit. The assassin, moreover, decides both when and where the hit will take place and how much he's to be paid for it. An underworld version of Raymond Chandler's Philip Marlowe, Dillon devotes himself utterly to the execution of his job; his standards won't be compromised. And the professionalism with which he explains the right way to kill a man wins him the Eddie Coyle assignment—on his own terms.

He also gets to stage the hit in his own way because of his reputation for accountability. A gangster who makes good on his word stands high in the underworld. As Jackie Brown will learn, one who reneges on an agreement will meet grief. He's told by Coyle after hedging on a promise to deliver guns, "once you say it's going to happen, *it's going to fucking happen*" (65). Jackie needs to learn this lesson. A businessman who defaults on his word may get fired; a defaulting mobster could die. Already hounded by the law, a thug can't let himself be bilked by one of his kind. A career in crime, we're meant to conclude, calls for more skill, patience, and dependability than one in business or the professions.

A line of work this obdurate and unforgiving polices itself. Twice, Coyle exchanges guns for cash in deals that end with the seller declining to count the money handed to him (89, 113). He and his business partner may have lied, exaggerated, and even threatened each other while negotiating their price. But once they agreed on a price, they made it law. No buyer of illegal guns will default on this sum; nor will he pay in counterfeit bills. The mob values the services of the supplier too much to cheat him. The supplier respects honor and trust because cheating will stain his image, let alone kill him. We're back in the realm of Adam Smith's textbook capitalism. Giving value for money and paying the right amount on time for goods and services promptly delivered builds healthy partnerships.

This confidence is crucial in the arms trade. A gangster needs guns to enforce his demands. But he has another reason to cultivate the good will of an weapons dealer. A conduit between supplier and client, the dealer, as both buyer and seller, has to transact business twice. He may also hold the weapons he deals for more time than his partners in crime, which increases his risk. Getting caught with an illegal machine gun by a federal officer means life in jail. Despite his youth, Jackie has an elite position in Boston's underworld, largely because of the pressure placed on him. He must meet quotas and deadlines while also maintaining quality control in order to please clients who aren't long on trust.

As Higgins would show in *Bomber's Law* and *At End of Day*, crooks and cops make up a society of their own despite standing, theoretically, anyway, on opposite sides of the law. Though vexing to the honest and the upright, this informal alliance makes sense. Both lawman and outlaw respect bravery, honesty, and toughness. But they also know that nothing saves lives like forethought, caution, and reserve. Prudence keeps crooks out of jail. Dave Foley's assessment of Jackie Brown, "He's a tough, smart kid" (121), honors Jackie's professionalism. This stance is typical. Any cop who underrates the criminals he's dogging will come up empty-handed. The better the criminal, the less he leaves to chance. Having departed the Massachusetts Cooperative Bank with their stash in hand in Chapter Twenty, Scalisi's team of robbers drive from the Bank's parking lot "quickly by not conspicuously so" (128). Then, according to plan, the car used to take the haul from the bank is *not* the one that moves it out of town.

Another sign of respect extended by crime-stoppers to criminals merits at least two references in the book. Agents will not lean too hard on their informers unless the informers are under arrest, where little pressure is needed. Grateful for what Coyle tells him in Chapter Two, Foley doesn't push him to name his source (15). In Chapter Twenty-Two, Wanda Emmett snitches her abusive lover Jimmy Scalisi to a state cop but resists the cop's efforts, which aren't that great anyway, to pry further information from her (141).

As is also shown in Sam Partridge's compliance when dealing with the hold-up men, criminals in Higgins usually get what they want. They're obeyed because organized crime represents a super-class, super-power, or Platonic form that subsumes the lesser realities of race, age, and social rank. Higgins makes the point through inflection. The subject of his 1972 novel is Eddie Coyle's circle of friends, who survive the badgered, fungible Coyle. The eponyms of Higgins's first three books, in fact, come before us in the possessive, not nominative, case, a device that diminishes them. They stay diminished. Although the titles, T*he Friends of Eddie Coyle, The Digger's Game,* and *Cogan's Trade* invoke a range of meanings, they all exalt crime at the expense of criminals. Kafka's belief that institutions survive by crushing their staffers comes to mind. Coyle dies, as will his murderer Dillon in *Cogan's Trade* (215).

The Patriot Game (1982) finds Jerry "Digger" Doherty back in jail. Though safe for now, the gang enforcer Jackie Cogan has a job that's unsuited to longevity. In fact, his death could occur seconds after the end of *Cogan's Trade*. The novel closes with a standoff, like Sam Shepard's 1980 play, *True West*. But the stakes are higher. Cogan and a fellow thug are poised to shoot each other, and both men know they could die on the spot. By pulling away from them before violence erupts, Higgins invites us to project our own hopes and fears into their standoff.

Regardless of the scene's outcome, Boston's underworld population figures to shrink by at least one. But the volume of criminal activity in the Hub will hold steady. The conversation between Jackie's legal defender and prosecutor that ends *Friends* argues, while also grazing the title of Higgins's next novel, *The Digger's Game* (1973), that the game continues. Only the players, or gamers, change. And such changes can happen without warning. For most of the second half of *Friends*, Coyle is living on borrowed time. Having inferred that only Coyle could have snitched him to the police, Jackie Brown swears revenge. Had Dillon not stopped Coyle, the self-composed, efficient Jackie would have done it, like Dillon, in a way heedless of the niceties of due process.

He'd have been following a code of justice that chews everything in its way. As soon as Dillon enters the book frightened, "hunched over to protect his stomach" (33), and pleading for help, the renewal associated with *The Phoenix*, a local newspaper he sees being peddled in Chapter Twenty-three (143), has already passed him by. His talk of committing suicide (41) is gratuitous. This death bringer already belongs to death. His separation or divorce from his wife (37) stands as one of the book's many examples of the clash between crime and living values, the death of "Digger" Doherty's priest-brother Paul in *The Patriot Game* being another.

The trailer, or mobile home, that bank robber and hired gun Jimmy Scalisi shares with Wanda while married to another woman symbolizes the rootlessness of criminal existence, a plight worsened by the constant movement a career in crime dictates. Appropriately, the car-savvy Higgins put Jackie Brown in a Roadrunner, which he's condemned to drive all over New England. Hungry (75) as well as tired, Jackie has reason to groan at the end of Chapter Twelve, "Jesus Christ . . . by the time I get fucking home tonight, it'll be midnight" (76). Though typically American in his proneness to action, he has taken both Yankee actionism and its attending can-do mentality to its raw edge. In Chapter Seventeen, he notes inwardly that he has just spent the past twenty-four hours driving 300 miles on four hours sleep (93). The one time he's seen sleeping, naturally in his car, he's arrested by the police. Higgins adds another brilliant touch here: the grab takes place near a railroad station, another emblem of transit and homelessness.

This instability and displacement thwart family wholeness. Gangsters live several lives concurrently, some of them patently middle class. In Chapter Five, Jackie and a customer bemoan the cost of automobile insurance. The imperatives of crime can also scramble middle-class routine. For though he's nobody's idea of a family man, Coyle wants to avoid jail so he can spend more time with his wife and kids (12-13). The same Jimmy Scal who talks about painting his home and taking his kids to church lives with a woman who's not his wife. His defection to Wanda's trailer in Orange points the clash between crime and family. Advisedly, the four bank robberies recounted in the book begin with the robbers invading the home of a married banker-father whose kids are living there with him and his wife.

Women lack identity in this brutal world. Shadow creatures, the wives of Dillon, Scalisi, and Coyle go unnamed, while those of the bankers who open their vaults for Scalisi's gang to plunder wait passively at home, unwilling captives who could die if the robberies fail. Coyle's wife has cares of her own. On show for less than half a page, she swaps barbed words with Coyle while watching television, her chief complaint being that she's always sent upstairs out of earshot when her husband uses the downstairs phone (157). She's married to a man she doesn't look at and is forbidden to listen to. Coyle can't be too careful about telephones. Ironically, his caution runs to waste. Many of his private phone conversations take place at the bar tended by Dillon, giving his future killer information about his whereabouts and thus making him easier to kill. Scalisi is also body-slammed by an action that erupts in the shadow of home. But the home is the trailer where he's living a sham marriage. Angry about being abused by him (he "likes to talk about fucking me in front of his friends" [141]), Wanda snitches him to the police.

Christmas in this dark, ferocious clime sullies its traditional joyful meaning in the same way that Scalisi and Wanda have cheapened the sacrament of marriage. By ending Chapters Two and Six with Dave Foley wishing an informer a merry Christmas (16, 42), Higgins foreshadows the shocks Christmas will suffer during the coming action. The shocks take different forms. The doomed banker Robert Biggers talks of the Christmas club promotions his bank is offering (123). But he's addressing the wife he has been deceiving, and he dies within an hour in the presence of his partner in adultery. Christianity, anchored in the birth of Christ, continues to make its presence felt, but, like the defining marks of Wanda's tie with Scalisi, in ways hostile to the forgiveness and charity encouraged by Christmas. Coyle remembers the childhood trauma of being whacked by a nun across the same knuckles the mob would crush years later (4-5). In Chapter Four, Dillon and Foley hear "a couple of Jesus screamers" (34) in downtown Boston who might be lamenting—or mocking--Coyle's pain.

The "good act of Contrition" (40) Dillon refers to minutes later either never takes place or goes unnoticed. The pigeons he calls "flying rats' (38) have driven out the dove of peace. In fact, the promise of salvation has waned by book's end, a reference to "late autumn" (151) in Chapter Sixteen clouding the hope put forth by Foley's Christmas greetings in Chapters Two and Six. Christmas has been sideswiped. The bank robber who dies in the aborted heist of Chapter 24 is called Donnie Goodweather (167). The Eucharistic associations put out by the volley of bullets that "chewed . . . up" (162) Donnie calls forth at least one more raid on Christian ritual. The setting of Jackie Brown's trial on 6

January, viz., Epiphany Day (181) has supplanted the god of love and peace with this avatar of discord and violence.

The emergence here of eschatology mires the book still deeper in the pits of damnation. Only Jackie appears in both the book's first and last chapters. Like the rattlesnake in Chapter Seven, that ancient symbol of betrayal, he's still roaming free at book's end. *Friends* endorses the belief, also held by Henry James, Graham Greene, and Peter Carey, that love invites betrayal. But it goes further. The absence of love makes betrayal the connection between people. It's also the staple of life. In our hard, fighting world, survival entails treachery; we can't stay alive without harming others, usually those closest to us. To his credit, Higgins doesn't show contempt or impatience for the unsympathetic souls who enact this sad heartbreaking drama. And it's his careful, well-judged technique that makes us care about their conflicts and hopes.

III

Friends uses the art of inter-cutting to create an aura of suspense and improvisation. It moves back and forth between both settings and groups of characters, developing cumulatively and nearly effortlessly. Dave Foley, the Treasury agent, for instance, uses three different informers we know of, two of whom, Dillon and the black man Deetzer, he pays a retainer. Coyle he doesn't pay, first, because he doesn't have to and, next, because he wants to keep Coyle mindful of his dearth of bargaining chips.

Repetition tempered by variation gives the book both flow and emphasis in other ways. In Chapter Eighteen, the sports fan Scalisi, who's first seen at a football game (in Chapter Three), complains that living in Orange, some two hours distance from Boston, has deprived him of watching Bruins hockey in person. The ice-loss equation gains force in the next chapter when Treasury cop Maury Walters has to give up his hockey tickets to work on the Jackie Brown case (116). The hockey game that *is* witnessed in person ends the growing irritation, but at a deadly price. "What a future he's got" (175), peals Eddie Coyle while admiring the puck-handling skills of Bruin Bobby Orr. Ironically, Coyle lacks a future himself. He gets so drunk at Boston Garden that he's an easy mark for the bullets that put him on a slab in an ice-cold morgue.

Friends gains in other ways from being experience driven rather than idea driven. Rhythm and variety support Higgins's description of the four bank jobs recorded in the novel. The tone is set even before the first job occurs. In Chapter Six, Foley and Dillon are talking outdoors in downtown Boston. The next chapter opens with a suburban family terrified by three armed men waiting for them on their living-room couch as they come downstairs for breakfast. The men have broken into the Partridges' home because Sam's duties include opening the bank they have planned to rob. The second robbery, which takes place the following week, though sharing many details of the first, including the identity of the perps, reaches us as a radio report in Chapter Fourteen (85). The third, coming in Chapter Twenty, reflects still more counterpoint. This heist, again performed by the same nylon-masked thugs who did the two earlier ones, unfolds as it's happening inside the bank.

The thugs have already entered the home of the bank officer and driven him to the bank, where they're all seen waiting for the time lock on the vault to open. Again, like Sam Partridge in Chapter Seven, the officer counsels prudence, compliance, and the shunning of heroics. But the heist fails because Bob Biggers signals the police, and two people die. Narrative tension has spiked. The robbers have become killers, creating both an urgency and a poetic justice that validate the outcome of the book's fourth and final robbery. Which is aborted; acting on Wanda's tip, the police are waiting at the banker's home. The thugs have walked into a trap, wearing their trademark nylon masks and, regrettably for them, carrying weapons. Their arrest displays Higgins's rare gift for channeling repetition into a coherent set of insights into motive and character to build a crescendo.

His steady hand, keen sensibility, and rare powers of observation also create revelations from the ephemera of moments. He's an accomplished miniaturist, his books, including *Friends*, often comprising a series of tableaux—short, clipped, monochromatic scenes—that build a pattern. After starting mid-scene, i.e., in the middle of an ongoing action, the tableau or episode will develop by means of dialogue, the word choice, rhythm, and speech intonations of which have won frequent praise. One of the many voices that have acclaimed Higgins's genius with dialogue booms from the *New Republic*: "Higgins has fashioned . . . novelistic speech out of the actual materials, and there's not a false note anywhere."[3] The genuineness the anonymous reviewer cites bespeaks the energy, concentration, and control that *Friends* upholds to its very end. It also helps lift the book from the shoals of minimalism. At issue is narrative stability. The friends noted in the book's title are all people we'd not want to extend friendship to. But, as in any other good novel, the last scene withholds any tidy moral, easy justice, or purity of motive. It counts in Higgins's favor that we're left with a bigger mystery at the end than the one that puzzled us in Chapter One.

The book's grip stems largely from Higgins's clear sense of where he wants to go and how he's going there. In an unpublished letter dated 16 December 1970 to the editor of Little, Brown Publishers he explained how the book's technique includes us readers in his quest:

It is . . . a difficult book. . . . I have tried to limit the reader's information about each episode as to what he would have perceived if he had happened to be present. This requires that the reader piece things together; he frequently receives information about individuals who are first denominated by their physical characteristics, and only later identified by name. . . . I chose this approach because it reflects . . . the fundamental uncertainty and fragmentation which participants in crime (cops and hoods) have about crime.[4]

Higgins puts us alongside his characters immediately. In the discussion between Coyle and Jackie Brown that comprises the first chapter, Coyle is designated throughout as "the stocky man" (e.g., 3, 5, 9). In Chapter Five, Jackie tells another client that he doesn't know Coyle's name (31). Jackie, by contrast, is referred to by name in the book's first sentence and thereafter because Coyle says he heard his name when he let it be known that he needed some weapons (3). Protocol dictates Coyle's anonymity in his dealings with Jackie. First, Coyle's wish to stay nameless is a courtesy Jackie (who's always called by his full name, perhaps to call attention to his brute amorality) gladly extends to him. As has been seen, the less Jackie knows about Coyle, the better for both of them in case the deal they're putting together goes wrong. Jackie can't give the police information he doesn't have.

And the police *are* on the scent, at one stage with Coyle's help. In Chapter Two, still known as "the stocky man" (e.g., 10), Coyle is talking to Dave Foley, here "the driver" (e.g. 10,16) of a Charger R/T that takes him to his meeting place with Coyle. Though referred to by Foley as "Eddie" (11), the stocky man isn't identified as Eddie Coyle till his third appearance in the book, in Chapter Four (25). But later meetings between him and Jackie in Chapters Ten and Fifteen show him reverting nominally to "the stocky man" (e.g., 65, 88). Authenticity has been served, Jackie still having found no reason to learn Coyle's name.

Identities aren't always masked. As a Treasury agent, Dave Foley can afford to show his face. The hoods he deals with want his help. Thus he goes from being "the driver' to "the agent" in the course of two paragraphs (15), and, in his next appearance, where he talks with a colleague in Chapter Four, he comes to us as "Dave" (25-8). Forget that his colleague never speaks his name. He needn't. Having perhaps worked with him for years, he thinks of Foley as "Dave." With Dillon, another crook, Foley goes by his last name (33) before relaxing into "Dave" (41) after several minutes of talk. He only emerges as "Dave Foley" (55) at the start of Chapter Eight, in which he'll meet a third informer, Deetzer, who calls him both "Foles" (56) and "Dave" (58). Foley had his reasons for telling Deetzer his name. His keeping them from *us* squares with Higgins's dramatic technique. We don't know any more about Foley or Coyle than the people talking to them do.

This immediacy almost makes us eyewitnesses to what's happening on the page. Elmore Leonard nailed it when he said famously of the book's pace and drive, "So this was how you do it" (Easiest, v). Bright, muscular, and well judged, *The Friends of Eddie Coyle* is a book you can keep re-reading. Eschewing messages, it both invites and resists interpretation. Each reading evokes new lines of thought, making us ponder afresh even the most familiar passages. Both sharp and authentic, it's a fine achievement. We leave it dazed, deeply moved, and feeling hard pressed to imagine a much better start to a writing career.

Notes

1. William McPherson, "More than a Thriller," *Washington Post*, 3 February 1972, B9.

2. Dated 16 December 1970, the letter is part of the Higgins Archive at the Thomas Cooper Library, University of South Carolina, Columbia, SC 29208.

3. "In Brief," *New Republic*, 8 April 1972, 21.

4. See note 2, above.

Conclusion

Higgins doesn't write counterfactual history. The battlefield casualties tallied in *Wonderful Years* and *Victories* describe his United States as the pitiful helpless giant created by the disasters of Watergate and the Vietnam War. Nor is help on the way. Any efforts on the parts of the student-radicals-turned-bank-robbers in *Outlaws* to promote social justice and economic equality during this shameful time only worsen the barbarism they've been trying to squelch. Set some 25 years after Vietnam, *At End of Day*, Higgins's last novel, describes a greater danger. When it came to marketable crops in the mid-1990s, there was one show in town, which everyone knew was narcotics. In both the poor, undeveloped countries of the world and the streets of America's big affluent cities, heroine and cocaine meant security, hard cash, and guaranteed credit.

Anchored in this turmoil, Higgins's fictional world is no friendly, inviting place where the quest for freedom brings happy results. His work is fed by sorrow as much as by wit, and usually sorrow wins out. It can seep into everything. A sharp student of both corporate and family dynamics, Higgins makes withholding husbands, missed connections, and losses common irritations. The frustration builds as his career moves forward. The 1986 short stories, "The Devil Is Real," and "Intentional Pass," together with "Bliss" (1988) and the novels *Wonderful Years* (1988) and *Sandra Nichols Found Dead* (1996) treat the pain of separation and divorce. The pain can flare up quickly, as Higgins makes clear in a passage from the title story of *The Easiest Thing in the World*: "[T]he easiest thing in the world is to take a man's wife from him if she feels . . . bored" (26).

Focusing this recklessness is Boston, a place dominated by the pursuit of money, power, and sex. Higgins's hometown rarely consoles or comforts. He never meant it to. He knows his turf, having studied it carefully, and can spot the slightest signs of change. Which usually mean danger; things mostly sour or run downhill for Higgins's protagonists. Perhaps his sorriest victim is Jerry Kennedy, first-person narrator and Higgins's alter-mind in four novels published between 1980-96. Sharp and sympathetic, Jerry is a guy's guy, someone you can share a nice meal with, sit next to at a ball game, or have represent you in court. But he's also awkward and self-questioning, never fully at ease with himself.

Higgins responds to his disquiet with insight, aware of its moral complexity and the human tragedy it invokes. Jerry worries about the same unconscious bonds between dread and love, sex and death, that riveted Freud. His forebodings take the form of feeling lost and out of sync; he even worries about actions *not* taken as time is running out on him. Like Higgins, who also has two degrees from Boston College, he turned forty-one in 1980, the publication date of *Defense*, his debut.

Even here, his lawyering, though a source of money and prestige, distracts him from the family he calls his top priority. Cultivating the image of success to promote business, he drinks Heineken beer, takes tennis lessons, and enjoys discussing the relative merits of greater Boston's exclusive private schools (KD 35); the action of *Sandra Nichols*, his last bow, peaks at such a school. He can spot a Gucci or a Bally loafer from across a room. Worst of all, he fails to see that his work has pulled him from the nest. A client's problems that will keep Jerry out past the dinner hour even cancel a family vacation in Chapter Eleven of *Kennedy for the Defense*. Inevitably, his wife, having eaten too many meals alone, finds ways to busy herself outside the home.

The problems that ensue are real, heartfelt, and urgent. But a swarm of technical blunders on Higgins's part flatten and trivialize them. Characters who spend too little time on the page or who never appear at all carry disproportionate thematic weight. Plot structure falls to pieces. In Chapter Fifteen of *Defense*, for instance, chance puts Jerry in the precise spot where he can overhear a discussion of immediate interest to him. Besides making us feel that Higgins is cheating, Jerry's eavesdropping puts us two removes from the action. The woes pile up. Elsewhere in the book, Higgins both tells us things we don't need to know and withholds vital information (e.g., 28). There are other signs that his concentration has slipped. In Chapter Seventeen, he introduces a subplot regarding the smuggling of drugs but soon drops it.

All of the Jerry Kennedy books misfire technically, probably because Higgins stands so close to their first-person narrator. He writes with more power and insight when dealing with gangsters. Loose, meandering monologues and disjointed subplots sap the vigor of *Penance for Jerry Kennedy*, and the flock of characters introduced in the book's closing chapters bespeak loss of narrative grip. Much of the dialogue in *Defending Billy Ryan* is either pedestrian or *faux*-tough. Lazy writing in the form of references to Kipling's "lesser breeds without the law" (48). the hissing "explicit expectation" (66), and paragraphs consisting of 200- and 150-word sentences following each other in close order (60-1) also sink *Penance*. Yet this same forlorn book also contains one of Higgins's freshest conceits. The face of a bleached blond introduced in Chapter Thirteen framing "blue eyes that over the years had seen too many nice things turn out badly" (112).

Such gems, though a source of delight, often hide inside mounds of verbal sludge. Unevenness dogged Higgins's whole writing career. But it didn't smudge his dedication or his energy. He took a great artistic risk by moving from the hard, assaultive protocols that won him commercial and critical successes in his first three novels. The other novels from the first half of his career show him, albeit often with little success, trying new skills. Jonathan Yardley found the talkiness in *City on a Hill* fatal; writing in *New Republic*, he called *City* "a novel in which almost nothing happens."[1] He wasn't thinking of Flaubert's pristine aims in *Madame Bovary*, either. This 1975 work about the grooming of a political candidate is sluggish, and most of the talk moves in tired circles. What's more, Higgins calls attention to this dullness. The book's last chapter finds the same two men addressing the topic they had broached at the outset. Despite a glut of chatter and nervous activity, little progress has been made. The talking heads in this hermetic, self-indulgent book have achieved little besides boring the reader. A PR man's gibe, four chapters from the end, "we were shoveling shit against the tide," (221), stands as Higgins's concession of having failed his readers.

But let's not write the book off as a total disaster. The missteps in Higgins, however damaging, furthered his artistic growth. Mostly educated professionals, i.e., lawyers, the people in *City* have more extended vocabularies and speak in longer sentences than did the Boston hoods of Higgins's first three books. Another contrast: their sentences obey grammatical laws, sometimes include foreign words, and host a syntax more inclusive of subordination than anything seen heretofore in Higgins. Women also play a bigger role in *City*—appearing more often on the page and saying more. Higgins's decision to put his characters in a fishing boat in the book's first scene also brings in a device repeated in *Dreamland*, *Penance*, and *Swan Boats*, that of developing key narrative events on water. *City* puts forth some keen insights, too. Addressing the question, so important in American presidential politics starting in the 1980s, of a candidate's image, a political handler talks "not of things as they are, but of things as they are perceived" (199).

Though sharp and prophetic, this idea lacks the plotting to support it and thus falls flat, as does much of *Dreamland*, a more distinguished failure of the 1970s. Written in the Jane Austen mode, *Dreamland* cuts deeper than its calm surfaces suggest. To use Philip Rahv's famous Redskin-Paleface dichotomy in *Image and Idea* (1949), which pits Walt Whitman's robust open-air poetry against the finicky self-conscious quest for absolute norms of behavior in Hawthorne and Henry James, *Dreamland* tends toward the glumness of paleface writing. Higgins's heavy investment in it shows. His most radical departure from the free-wheeling, hang-loose ambience of *Eddie Coyle* and its two immediate successors, it traffics in repressiveness and civilized mantraps.

It's also shamelessly intellectual, quoting Yeats (106), Marvell (162), and A.H. Clough (180). Even its narrating voice has roots in western literature, harking to that of *Doctor Faustus*. In Thomas Mann's kingpin 1946 novel, a timid, conventional soul records the doings of a high-flyer but often without understanding all he reports. Compton Wills's confused voice helps weave the conversations he reports into an elegant, multi-leveled narrative, but, perforce, without the wonderfully ironic effects found in *Doctor Faustus*. *Dreamland*, though, survives this failing. Lacking visceral appeal, the novel feels weary and aimless, leaving it an art curiosity—and a mistake that helped Higgins long term.

*

The 1980s and 1990s saw Higgins turning to the novel of suburban unrest, or suburban literary Gothic, identified with Richard Yates and the two Johns, Cheever and Updike. Suburban Boston in Higgins is a place of empty social bonds, crass materialism, and heavy drinking. *Impostors* (1986), with its complicated real estate and media deals, statutory rape charge and election-year chicanery, builds a rich, many-faceted plot burnished by smart writing. The book provides other rewards. The attention it pays to animal-rights activism, gays, and the tendency of the law to ignore the hurts suffered by the lower classes both makes the novel stylishly contemporary and reveals, in Higgins, a moral passion, some of which takes the form of tough self-questioning.

Speaking of the witch he just finished representing in a divorce case, a puzzled, angry lawyer in *Impostors* says, "You know what I've done to John Flaherty to date. . . ? You know what I've done to a perfectly nice man whom I'd probably like, if I didn't represent his wife, whom I don't like at all? I have come pretty near to destroying his life" (354). In this novel in which the police shut off investigations that could damage their chiefs, Higgins rehearses the injustices bred by the power structure. Connie Gates is refined, socially accomplished, and talented. But, in Higgins's update of Henry James's down-at-heel sophisticates, she's also broke. Connie is one of many of Boston's educated divorced professionals. The chore of maintaining ties with her married friends, mostly thirty-something soccer moms, is defeating her. She and these friends, some of whom she has known since childhood, lack common interests. She's starved for social outlets elsewhere, too. Having also lost custody of her small son, she has to fight a tendency to drink, to spend money she doesn't have, and to bed-hop.

Sexual promiscuity in women becomes a major trope in *Wonderful Years*, a book in which two sisters have serial sex with the same HIV-infected man. But the book's most gripping female figure must be the bipolar sixty-year-old Nell Farley, who was based, according to Erwin H. Ford, on Higgins's "manic-depressive, paranoid, schizophrenic, alcoholic' first wife, Betty (34, n.44). *Wonderful Years* has a wide sweep. Like *A Choice of Enemies* and *Outlaws* before it, it describes the toil of securing contracts for public work projects like resurfacing highways, installing television cable systems, and building parking lots for schools. A contractor's work is a nightmare. Before any machinery can be flat-bedded to a job site, lawyers must work out details of insurance and bonding. Other slog includes appeasing conservationists, equal opportunity officers, and health-department inspectors of field toilets.

This work has an ugly side. It starts with buying drinks, dinners, and baseball tickets for delegates and selectmen. But the pols who assess bids for state contracts want more. They expect kickbacks, jobs for their friends, and sometimes even the right to be serviced sexually. Contractor Ken Farley has found himself trapped in an upside-down version of tragedy, as it's defined by Robert Frost; something terrible is happening, and nobody's to blame. Like Mark Baldwin in *Impostors*, Farley has to sin to stay in business. His duty to hundreds of loyal, hard-working employees has mired him in sleaze.

This quagmire recalls the dilemma of banker Sam Partridge in *Eddie Coyle*, who conspires with bank robbers to save human lives. The depiction of both Sam's and Ken Farley's needing to protect the bad to fend off the worst invokes a key feature of Higgins's art: men interest Higgins more than women, who tend to vague personalities or types, which leaves them case illustrations rather than fully rounded individuals. This bias changes in *Wonderful Years*. Despite all the attention paid by Higgins to the hard practical male work of getting things done, the core of the novel occupies emotional ground where reason counts for little.

Wonderful Years opens with a diligent, craftsmanly description if a rundown Berkshire resort. Its first paragraph fits the resort inside its geographical surroundings. By the second paragraph, the weight of physical detail has already made us worry if Higgins might have misapplied his stylistic rigor and amplitude. He has patiently recovered the physical features of the hotel—the doors, the flagstone floor of the foyer and lobby, and the registration desk. But he's not sacrificing plot to stylistic indulgence. The tablecloths in the dining room, "frayed at the edges and mended in places" (1), denote a wear-and-tear that intensifies in the rusty, leaking framework and soiled walls seen in the next paragraph (1). Description stays thematic. The solarium and its "ominous plants with broad leaves yellowed and browned at the edges," air "heavy and moist," and flooring "alternately slick and sticky underfoot" (2), all give Higgins's multi-sensory imagery a Chandleresque foreboding.

This creepy place is presided over by an angry-eyed parrot known to bite anyone foolish enough to feed it by hand; one character calls it the devil (67). And the person most closely identified with it? A look into literary history makes the question worth asking. Flaubert's Félicité in "A Simple Story" is simple herself; she exists to serve others. She also loves her pet parrot, whom she has stuffed by a taxidermist after its death. The bird has become an image of the Holy Ghost to her. This imputed sanctity calls forth the devilishness attributed to the parrot at Higgins's Foothills Inn. The attributor, selfish, devious Nell Farley, plagues her cadre of keepers and retainers. Crafty and calculating during her moments of clarity, she alternates moments of hysteria and deep spiritual insight when she loses grip—unless these wild moments show her confronting reality head-on.

Her wildness is painful to witness. When she's not cursing the husband she claims to have betrayed her, she wants to rejoin him. And perhaps she has grounded her refusal to divorce Ken Farley, not in spite, as everyone believes, but in the Christian virtues of love and forgiveness. Her ability to retain her faith despite great suffering has made her a fool saint; lacking common sense, she dies from hypothermia after fleeing into the snow. Perhaps like the heroine of Patrick White's *Aunt's Story* (1948), she's punished for risking a purity and intensity off limits to humankind save the odd religious mystic. That the Australian White's itinerant aunt ends her pilgrimage in America reminds us of Nell Farley's place in American literary history. That place harbors the sad and the desperate. Like the narrators of Charlotte Perkins Gilman's "Yellow Wallpaper' (1892) and James's *Turn of the Screw* (1898), Nell suffers from seclusion, sexual suppression, and psychological breakdown.

Higgins's artistic rendering of her pain is more in character than most of his readers might expect. Throughout his career, Higgins maintained an interest in cooking, interior domestic design, and the joys of music—activities that come easier to women than to men. Would that he had converted this interest to artistic gains. Blame the disconnect on him. Had he dramatized this flair rather than voicing it in long unassimilated passages of reportage, he'd have improved his art. As they stand, many of his descriptions in *Wonderful Years* distract as much as they illuminate. By contrast, the tender, quiet revelations evoked by the passages dealing with Nell Farley stem from authorial restraint. Painful for Higgins to write because of their roots in his marital woes, the Nell Farley passages avoid the malady of overwriting.

This well-judged lyricism is rare in Higgins's middle and late work, where his passion for inclusiveness and explicitness frequently cloud his writing. This verbal overload goes hand in glove with knowingness. A blizzard of descriptive verbiage results when he opts for the big sweep into family history, demographics, or, as in *Victories*, the bonds between lumberjacking, logging, and the building industry in nineteenth-century New England. A later novel whose fecundity is more burdensome than exhilarating is *Swan Boats at Four*. This minutely considered work has a dense, self-conscious articulation that gives it a high intelligence. Like its subtly inflected prose, the complex menace it unravels calls to mind the late Henry James. Jamesian too are the motives into motives to be weighed along with the reactions to reactions to be deciphered. Along with Ken Farley of *Wonderful Years*, *Swan Boat*'s David Carroll shows Higgins growing increasingly fond of contractors and bankers as his career moves ahead (creatures of plotting, two bankers get killed in *Eddie Coyle*). Deregulation, regional takeovers of other banks, and the demands made on him by SEC inspectors have been making David sweat to meet payroll deadlines.

The threat of having his bank seized by the Feds has been ransacking him. His wife says he's "close to exhaustion" (130), and a sharp-eyed stranger describes him as someone "who used to be in pretty decent shape, 'fore he stopped working out not too long ago" (33). But rather than relaxing him, the ocean cruise his wife mandates bogs him down in increasing levels of complexity, nuance, and ambiguity. His downfall, though, could owe more to Kafka than to James, a possibility invited by the phrase, "the easiest thing in the world," which appears in one of Kafka's most famous tales, "A Hunger Artist."[2] A bureaucracy as cruel and inscrutable as any found in Kafka's Prague has closed in on David, darkening both his high-prestige job and his home. Acting as if he deserves this nightmare, he speeds it by drinking, wenching, and abandoning his bank at a time when a team of federal officers plan to swoop down on it and grab his ledger books.

Higgins's own book blocks our way to David. It idles, stops and starts, and then slips into reverse, a glut of back-story jamming its gears. A warning sign comes in Chapter Six in the form of a cameo biography of a dead man whose wife died before the book's present-tense action (57). The following chapter is mugged by Higgins's lazy adaptation of the Jamesian voice. Straight out of "The Beast in the Jungle" (i.e., the description of John Marcher's reunion with May Bartram) comes David's reaction to a young lady he'd not seen for years:

> There was a new wintry throatiness in the timbre of her voice; it had to be deliberate. She'd installed it since he'd known her. She was the kind of a woman who decided early that she wanted it to be there, and she had put it there on purpose, probably defensively. (64)

The words that pass between David and Melissa Murray keep harking to those of James's 1903 story:

> "Ahh," he said inartfully, so you *are* the same one, in fact. How many years has it been?"
> "Eight," she said promptly, "exactly eight years. But you see, I didn't forget you." (66)

Another Jamesian touch, perhaps Higgins's rebuke to himself for coasting, comes in Chapter Fifteen when a Beacon Hill grandee watches a fellow clubman watching a vagrant rooting through trash. Plenty in *Swan Boats* is discardable; a single paragraph in Chapter Eleven harbors the solecism, "feeling at somewhat of a loss" and the awful-sounding "initially mildly" (123). These flubs make it clear that the Higgins of *Swan Boats* didn't use disruptive narrative techniques to serve some hidden postmodern purpose. As usual, the high drama of certain scenes in *Swan Boats* stands out. But because this mannered, over-explicit book stumbles so often, it loses its way. Higgins's own awareness of this problem showed in his decision to return in his next novel, *Sandra Nichols*, to the Jerry Kennedy series, where, he hoped, his familiarity with the series' narrator and his beat, Boston's legal world, might control him.

Higgins's best book of the 1980s, *A Choice of Enemies*, scores high because it avoids the self-conscious mannerism of *Swan Boats*. Much of the book's bite comes from Bernie Morgan. Ironically, this pugnaciously non-literary work may have gotten its first push from Edwin O'Connor's *Last Hurrah*. But instead of basing his 1984 novel on Boston's former mayor, James Michael Curley, Higgins used John Forbes Thompson, who, like Morgan, served as Speaker of the House of Representatives for the Commonwealth of Massachusetts (OW 125). Ford has rehearsed the similarities between theses two hard-chargers.

Thompson was wounded in action in World War II, a hardship he'd later use to get elected to Massachusetts's House of Representatives. Once installed, he climbed quickly. His skills as a debater and a deal maker helped him become the youngest majority leader ever of the House, even though he never took a law degree. Greater knowledge of (and respect for) the law would have helped him. At the time of his death, this boozer was also under indictment by the grand jury for taking bribes (Ford 216).

Though Morgan's career doesn't parallel Thompson's exactly, it traces the same curve. What's most important, both men are the same kind of "mongrel American" (Ford 217) whose crushing banality wins battle after political battle. No warped, ruthless monster, Morgan is impelled by the sheer force of his commonness. His rough edges don't bother him. This "fat . . . arrogant . . . alcoholic crook" (CE 9) lives by his own rules. He divides his free time between two women named Maggie, and, "[d]irty fighter" (15) that he is, he backs down to nobody. A young Latino who made the mistake of scratching the paintwork on his Cadillac Seville leaves the incident on a stretcher with injuries to his skull, pelvis, wrist, and nose (CE 17). Any political foe will find Morgan dangerous, too. Quickly, he'll deploy his managerial skills, common sense, and willingness to smash anyone who gets in his way.

During an interview with a head of an under-funded hospital, he contrasts himself with Plato, who saw enlightenment in the Idea of the Good (275). Morgan, on the other hand, knows that the implementation of liberty and equality calls for dirty work. Instead of scanning the heavens, he toils in the trenches. Machiavelli has influenced him even more than the pragmatic Aristotle. Rather than wanting to change the world, he has learned how it works. Social problems, he admits, may not be solved, but, thanks to his roughhouse populism, they can be managed. Morgan controls the courts, the legislature, and the Treasury of Massachusetts because he looks people in the eye, shakes their hands, buys drinks, and doles out a few bucks that he extorts from contractors and job-seekers.

The civic idealism and high-mindedness he rhapsodizes about to voters fade into the everyday practice of government, a hodgepodge of trade-offs and hidden agendas, swindles, and threats. Yet this "benign scoundrel" (Ford 217) has proved that vice sustains as it corrupts. If the incarnation of an idea mars the idea's purity, it also delivers blood and sinew, rescuing it from the nowhere of abstraction, where it's useless, anyway.

Choice is a good book but not a great one, despite its smattering of great scenes. It's sort of a field guide to the roughneck ways of the Irish-American politicians who ousted their Ivy League WASP predecessors from public service in greater Boston. This paradigm in Higgins's hands has all the irregularity of life. Even though Morgan looks Irish and drinks like an Irish politician, he's only a quarter Irish (280). His Scotch-English bloodlines distance him from his Irish constituents, helping him see them clearly without buying into their self-images. He has the advantages of the semi-outsider. Like the Minnesotan Scott Fitzgerald in Ivy League society and the English-reared Raymond Chandler in

L.A., he shows that observing a scene at one remove sharpens the comedy in it. This perspective also tempers the argument that, despite the wealth of religious materials in the Higgins canon, his people, like many of those in Joyce's *Dubliners*, inhabit a spiritual void.

These people are limited, mostly because they're too busy clinching deals, trying to avoid the slammer, or, in some cases, foiling a would-be assassin to look into the dark interiors of their lives. Absent from the canon is the spiritual unworthiness plaguing Graham Greene's demonic heroes or even the sordid religiosity of Jean Genet. But *Choice* finds Higgins not only facing unreason and nightmare but also putting this counter-world inside a religious frame. In Chapter Thirteen, Morgan dreams that his mother is attending a mass celebrating his installation as a priest. But his words aren't priest-like, and the episode ends with a sharp image, Higgins saying of the priest shocked by Morgan's raffishness, "Wallace's face went white, and his lips almost disappeared" (131).

*

In *Impostors* as well as *Choice*, Higgins's legal training helped him scotch any boondoggle foisted by influence peddlers on the public. But this lore, though impressive, also bypasses problems caused by the seemingly disconnected nature of his achievements. Books like *City on a Hill*, *A Year or so with Edgar*, and *The Mandeville Talent* seem like so much marking time, while *Swan Boats* and *Sandra Nichols* misfire most of the way. Despite its virtues, a Higgins novel *can* say too much about itself and not enough about the reality we're all struggling to make sense of. Reading the canon is a chore. But the it does yield solid rewards. Though lacking the range of Balzac or Joyce, within his tighter frame Higgins worked to impressive depth. His model here is Henry James. As in James, almost everything in Higgins lies in the mode of expression. He scrutinizes, selects, and arranges with great care. Sometimes the process defeats him. But when he's on his game, he can make his sentences a joy, doing in a phrase what most literary fiction (including his own) usually takes two pages of workshop-conditioned narrative to plod through.

What enables him to evoke a setting, convey the essence of a situation, and glimpse the inmost heart of a character with such economy, is his mastery of the intimate detail. An ace observer, he uses specifics both to build a mood and to soak the reader in the daily rhythms and routines of his people. There's a lyricism at work here, a fine attentiveness to everyday existence, achieved with casual speed and authority. That's magic for you. And it's spun by Higgins's command of colloquial speech. Slang and cliché in Higgins poeticize the prosaic.

The impromptu talk in *The Digger's Game* (1973) brings home this lyricism. Higgins doesn't let the Digger's efforts to pay his gambling debts dominate the book. Nor does he build suspense or shock with violent images, as do most crime writers. No cops-and-robbers chase permeates the script; the theft of several hundred thousand dollars worth of furs takes less than a page to report; the book's one gun-fight is described in such monotonous sentence rhythms that it can't grip us.

Presented more vividly is the drive to the potential murder-victim's home— the nervous chatter, the tricks the impending murder plays with the appetite, digestion, and bowels, and also the plain, dumb waiting. The impact of *The Digger's Game* doesn't come from ideas or physical action but from the intimate view the book gives of Boston's underworld. The toning-down of dramatic climaxes also blocks the formation of a shapely, driving plot. But it does let the people be themselves. Freed from the controls exerted by plot, they can gossip about local politics, relive old adventures, or reminisce about gangster-chums now dead or in jail. Yet *Digger* isn't random or static. The dangers shadowing the characters' most routine movements create an urgency that steers the action.

As this approaches great writing, it also builds fiction of a significant and durable sort. A Higgins novel isn't so much a substitute for great literature as an important aspect of it. Its eddies, asides, and leftover bits of life both fashion an era and cohere as a universe of its own. Forget critical definitions; Higgins is a genius whose art transcends regionalism. When you keep turning pages because you want to know what happens next, you've surrendered to the craft of the novelist, not the talented oddball.

Higgins's whipcord, on-the-spot artistry captures the gleeful, harsh rowdiness of urban America that also fascinated Walt Whitman and recurs in both the freaky banality of Chuck Close's large portrait heads and the news photos that Andy Warhol silk-screened onto canvas. Such descriptions of the urban heebie-jeebies remind us that Higgins didn't sacrifice character and plot to language; no decadent, he. Conventional categories of fiction say little about narrative development in his work. His people have drives rooted in who they are rather than in motives dictated by plot structure. As in Tolstoy, inner life in Higgins is much less a function of narrative than one of existence. He has mastered the comic rhythms of Boston's underworld. When he reports the conversation of crooks, he stands alone; nobody does it better. The dialogue is clear, crisply stylized, and pungent as garlic. Everything moves. Sometimes matters take a comic direction, the people generating some seriously funny scenes. Heed these scenes. Humor can celebrate life's incongruity; but it's also a way to get to the bottom of things.

Disarming and subverting reader expectations, it incites chilling, thought-provoking moments in Higgins. The deep structure in his work fuses the lawyer, the priest, and the thug. What results from this fusion is a bizarre hour-glass morality. The lawyer and the priest both see in the thug a reflection of their own wayward youths. The thug grudgingly concedes that he must mend his thuggish ways.

This tension fuels one of Higgins's most humanly truthful scenes, i.e., the last-chapter meeting between the brothers Paul and Jerry, or the Digger, Doherty in *The Digger's Game*. The meeting combines the openness and the secrecy marking most fraternal bonds. But the openness comes from Paul, with Jerry hiding behind a wall of secrecy and lies. Higgins's instinct for the off-center detail provides an added sting. For Paul is both Jerry's brother and, as a priest, his spiritual father, aggravating the tension between the men; Paul even addresses Jerry only partly in jest as "my son" (209). The Oedipal note isn't gratuitous. Jerry flusters when he learns that his wife Agatha had been drinking with Paul for two hours while dressed in a nightgown; "They don't cut off your goddamned equipment when you put the collar on" (209), Jerry grumps.

Paul is grumpy, too, because Jerry broke his promise to give up crime in exchange for Paul's gift of $3000 earlier in the book. The sulks dissolve with Paul's exit from his brother's Dorchester home, giving way to the jealousy that seized Jerry at his homecoming. But the jealousy shows a raw edge. The knowledge that a scantily clad Agatha chatted over drinks with Paul for two hours now stirs the Digger's lust—and perhaps hers. A rare finale in the history of crime fiction shows her and Jerry preparing to make love at book's end. Higgins's discretion here is admirable. It's also typical. Rather than pretending to understand the inner lives of his people, he describes effects and outcomes. He prefers conveying the texture of lived experience to the crafting of neat conclusions. Certain sides of his people remain mysterious, even to the people themselves, and the books leave them, appropriately, in the midst of life. But they're not abandoned to indeterminacy. Even inside the one's family of origin, Higgins has inferred, sex takes place in the shadow of money.

Higgins's treatment of such dynamics calls to mind one of fiction's main goals—understanding the other; in this case, a Boston priest and his gangster brother. Does the attainment of this understanding rankle? The lives led by most of Higgins's people are wretched, lacking in purpose and devoid of the warmth and fun that give human existence value. This distress carries forward. There's something strange and menacing at the heart of Higgins's work. Perhaps so many of his characters repel us because of the insecurity that keeps dogging them. Richard Beardsley noted this anxiety in his *Louisville Times* review of *The Friends of Eddie Coyle*. In this "taut, sordid, frightening story," Beardsley said with great wit, "Higgins makes the criminal element seem everywhere."[3] He's not complaining. Good fiction helps us feel what its people feel, no matter how much they differ from us.

Many of the changes recorded in Higgins depict loss, breakdown, even death. Change comes quickly. A minute after standing on solid ground, one of his people is reeling on mist. Nor does the luckless character feel cheated or maligned. Inside every monstrous ego in Higgins lies a trembling, damaged one. It can take time for the vulnerability to surface. But Higgins takes us significantly closer to grasping it than we were. Marianne Moore's telling poets to create imaginary gardens inhabited by real toads presumes the thematic gold straddling the frontier between fiction and reality. Like Moore's ideal poet, Higgins dramatizes not only the neglected but also the repressed. His ability to shake the ground under our feet grips us at the outset. And once he's hooked us, he can use what we're willing to accept to make us look at what we fear.

His art touches our senses and emotions as much as it does our minds. Its strength is evident. Thanks to the risks it takes, it often looks fresh. Most of the time, its range and resonance also outstrips what the competition is putting out. On the debit side, it includes some missteps, and it includes them too often. But we shouldn't fret. These flaws, though regrettable, don't mar the truth that George V. Higgins attained the preeminence projected by that smashing first sentence of his debut novel, *The Friends of Eddie Coyle*: "Jackie Brown at twenty-six, with no expression on his face, said that he could get some guns" (3).

Notes

1. Jonathan Yardley, "What Happens?" *New Republic*, 12 April 1975, 29.
2. Franz Kafka, "A Hunger Artist," trans. Willa and Edwin Muir, *The Complete Stories*, ed. Nahum S. Glatzer, Foreword by John Updike (New York: Schocken, 1983), 270.
3. Richard Beardsley, "'The Friends of Eddie Coyle' tell a taut, frightening story of crime," *Louisville Times*, 28 January 1972, 12 C).

Selected Bibliography

Works by George V. Higgins (chronological)

Novels
The Friends of Eddie Coyle. New York: [Alfred A.] Knopf, 1972. London: Secker and Warburg [1972].
The Digger's Game. New York: Knopf, 1973. London: Secker and Warburg [1973].
Cogan's Trade. New York: Knopf, 1974. London: Secker & Warburg [1974].
A City on a Hill. New York: Knopf, 1975. London: Secker & Warburg [1975].
The Judgment of Deke Hunter. Boston: Little, Brown: An Atlantic Monthly Press Book, 1976. London: Secker & Warburg [1976].
Dreamland. Boston and Toronto: Little, Brown: An Atlantic Monthly Press Book, 1977. London: Secker & Warburg [1977].
A Year or So with Edgar. New York: Harper & Row, 1979. London: Secker & Warburg [1979].
Kennedy for the Defense. New York: Knopf, 1980. London: Secker & Warburg [1980].
The Rat on Fire. New York: Knopf, 1981. London: Secker & Warburg, 1981.
The Patriot Game. New York: Knopf, 1981. London: Secker & Warburg [1982].
A Choice of Enemies. New York: Knopf, 1984. London: Secker & Warburg [1984].
Penance for Jerry Kennedy. New York: Knopf, 1985. [London:] [Andre] Deutsch [1985].
Impostors. New York: Henry Holt, 1986. [London:] Deutsch [1986].
Outlaws. New York: Henry Holt, 1987. [London:] Deutsch [1987].
Wonderful Years, Wonderful Years. New York: Henry Holt, 1988. [London:] Deutsch [1988].
Trust. New York: Henry Holt, 1989. [London:] Deutsch [1989].
Victories. New York: Henry Holt, 1990. [London:] Deutsch [1991].
The Mandeville Talent. New York: Henry Holt: A John Macrae Book, 1991. [London:] Deutsch [1991].
Defending Billy Ryan. New York; Henry Holt: A John Macrae Book, 1992. [London:] Little, Brown [1993].

129

Bomber's Law. New York: Henry Holt: A John Macrae Book, 1993. [London:] Little, Brown [1994].
Swan Boats at Four. New York: Henry Holt: A John Macrae Book, 1995. [London:]Little, Brown [1995].
Sandra Nichols Found Dead. New York: Henry Holt: A John Macrae Book, 1996. [London:] Little, Brown, 1996.
A Change of Gravity. New York: Henry Holt: A John Macrae Book, 1997. [London:] Little, Brown [1999].
The Agent. New York: Harcourt Brace, 1998. [Harpenden (UK): No Exit] 2000.
At End of Day. New York: Harcourt, 2000.

Short Story Collections
The Sins of the Fathers.. London: Deutsch, 1988.
The Easiest Thing in the World: The Uncollected Fiction of George V. Higgins. Ed. Matthew J. Bruccoli, introd. Robert B. Parker. New York: Carroll & Graf, 2004.

Nonfiction
The Friends of Richard Nixon. Boston: Little, Brown, 1975.
Style Versus Substance: Kevin White and the Politics of Illusion. New York: Macmillan, 1984.
The Progress of the Seasons: Forty Years of Baseball in Our Town. New York: Henry Holt, 1989.
On Writing: Advice to Those Who Write to Publish (or Would Like To). New York: Henry Holt, 1990. [London:] Bloomsbury [1991].

Uncollected Short Stories (chronological)
"No Traveler Returns." *Stylus: The University Quarterly of Boston College,* 73 (November 1959), 44-50.
"All Day Was All There Was." *Arizona Quarterly,* 19 (Spring 1963), 23-36.
"Witness: Something of a Memoir." *Massachusetts Review* 10 (Summer 1969), 596-602.
"Mass in the Tine of War." *Cimarron Review,* September 1969, 73-81.
"Something Dirty You Could Keep." *Massachusetts Review,* 10 (Autumn 1969), 631-44.
Old Earl Died Pulling Traps. Columbia, SC: Bruccoli Clark, 1984. [Included in *The Easiest Thing in the World,* 138-63.]
"A Martini for Father McBride." *Michigan Quarterly Review,* 37 (Winter 1998), 101-13.
"The Wrong Man," *Memories: The Magazine of Here and Now.* Spring 1998, 67-9.
"An Interview with Diane Fox," *Sewanee Review.* 107 (Winter 1999), 7-17.

Articles and Essays (chronological)
"Witness: Something of Myself." *Massachusetts Review,* 10 (Summer 1969), 596-602.
"The Private Eye as Illegal Hero." *Esquire,* December 1972, 348, 350-1.
"Afterword," James Ross, *They Don't Dance Much.* ed. Matthew J. Bruccoli (1940; Carbondale and Edwardsville, IL 1975), 297-302.
"Sentencing: The Problems of Individuation." *Trial: The National Legal Newsmagazine* 14 (April 1978), 42-4.
"Professor Richardson et al.: A New England Education." *New England Journal of Public Policy* 1 (Summer, Fall 1985), 37-46.

"Preface: A Man of Measured Discontents—John O'Hara and His Losses." John O'Hara, *Gibbsville, PA: The Classic Stories*. Ed. Matthew J, Bruccoli. New York: Carroll & Graf, 1992, 11-16.

Interviews (chronological)
Bannon, Barbara A. "Publisher's Weekly Interviews George V. Higgins." *Publisher's Weekly*, 203, n. 15 (1973), 26-7.
Brady, John. "The Writer's Digest Interview: George V. Higgins." *Writer's Digest*, December 1975, 24-9, 50-5.
Carlin, Margaret. "Boston Brawler." Rocky *Mountain* [Denver] *News Sunday Magazine/Books*, 27 July 1986, 23(M).
Doyle, Brian. "My Lunch with George." *Boston College Magazine*, 50 (Spring 1991), 22-30.
Williams, John. *Into the Badlands: Travels through Urban America*. London: Paladin-Grafton, 1991. 194-206.
Bondil, Pierre, facilitator, "Wonderful Times: Part One: George V. Higgins talks about his writing career to Pierre Bondil," *C[rime] A[nd] D[etective] S[tories]*37, May 2000, 29- 33.
— "Wonderful Times: Part Two: George V. Higgins talks abut his books to Pierre Bondil," *CADS*, 38, November 2000, 7-13.

The Higgins Archive
"Boston writer's archive finds new home at the University of South Carolina." *USC News*. 16 February 2004; *http://uscnews.sc.edu/lib045.html.*; 3 May 2004.

Checklist
[Bruccoli, Matthew J.] *The Books of George V. Higgins: A Checklist of Editions and Printings*. University of South Carolina Libraries, 2000.

Criticism and Commentary
Anderson, Roger K. "Novel presents a basket full of baddies." *Dallas Morning News*, 29 June 1986, 11(C).
Beardsley, Richard. 'The Friends of Eddie Coyle' tell a taut, frightening story of crime," *Louisville Times*, 28 June 1972, 12(C).
Binyon, T.J., "Crime File," *TLS*, 19 June 1987, 668.
Boot, Max. "Police-Beat Writer Spins City Tales," *Christian Science Monitor*, 22 September 1992, 12.
Bruccoli, Matthew J., "Editor's Note," George V. Higgins, *The Easiest Thing in the World*, ix-x.
Campbell, Robert. "A Perfect Sales Pitch." *Washington Post*. 22 October 1989, 5(X).
Carmichael, C.M. "The law: a fuzzy line to tread," *Christian Science Monitor*, 2 March 1972, 10.
— "A convincing argument for equity in these two novels by policemen," *Houston Post*, 16 April 1972, 13.
Christian, George. "Trouble in Boston," *Houston Chronicle*, 15 January 1989, 22, 25.
Coffey, Warren. "Flannery O'Connor," *Commentary*, 40, no. 5 (November 1965) 93-99.
Desilva, Bruce. "Get out if Jail Free," *New York Times Book Review*, 20 August 2000, 15.
Dretzka, Gary. "The Crimes of their lives," *Chicago Tribune*, 20 September 1987, 14(7).

— "Trust George Higgins to weave a winner," *Chicago Tribune*, 28 November 1989, 5(14).

Dyer, Richard. "Higgins Hones His Touch," *Boston Globe*, 19 September 1997, 2(D1).

— "Higgins makes sport of killing an agent," *Boston Globe*, 19 January 1999, 2(E).

— "George V. Higgins at Dusk," *Boston Sunday Globe*, 7 May 2000, 2(M1).

Flagg, Michael. "Francis and Higgins: Fiction Sporting and Tough," *[Raleigh] News and Observer*, 18 May 1986, 4(D).

"A Foot on the Ground," *New Statesman*, 13 August 1982, 22.

Ford, Erwin H., II. "Expiation Ritual in the Crime Novels of George V. Higgins," Ph. D. diss., State University of New York at Buffalo, 1988. A pioneering yet sophisticated look at major social and religious issues in Higgins.

— "Higgins Adds New Touches of Humanity," *Buffalo News*, 4 December 1988, 13(E).

Galligan, Edward L. "Henry James among the Cops in Boston," *Sewanee Review* 102 (Spring 1994), 181,

— "George V. Higgins 1939-1999," *Sewanee Review* 108 (Winter 2000), 148.

Gowrie, Grey. "Profanity behind the tea parties," *[London] Sunday Telegraph*, 12 November 1989, 18.

"In Brief." *New Republic,*" 8 April 1972, 21.

Johnson, Anne Janette. "Prime Elves are gleaned from Eavesdropping on Impostors," *Detroit Free Press*, 6 July 1986, 7(C).

Just, Ward. "Guns and Roses," *Boston Globe*, 19 December 2004, 3d ed., 6(K).

Kaplan, Frank L. "Not for the Casual Reader of Crime Novels," *Rocky Mountain* [Denver] *News*, 5 November 2004, 27(D).

Lehmann-Haupt, Christopher, "You're Dead, He Explained," *New York Times*, 25 January 1972, 33.

Leonard, Elmore, "Introduction," *The Friends of Eddie Coyle*. (1972: New York: Henry Holt: Owl, 1995), v-vii.

Levenston, E.A. "Literary Dialect in George V. Higgins's 'The Judgment of Deke Hunter," *English Studies*, 62 (1981), 358-70. A cunning, systematic analysis of GVH's prose.

Lewis, Peter. "Boston Burning," *TLS*, 5 June 1981, 640. The sharpest review ever of a Higgins book.

Mano, D. Keith. "Boston Laconic," *National Review*, 7 June 1974, 685.

— "Getting Better All the Time," *National Review*, 18 May 1984, 50-1.

McPherson, William. "More than a Thriller," *Washington Post*, 3 February 1973, 9(B).

Merritt, Robert. "Writers Try to Break away from Stereotypes," *Richmond Times*, 15 June 1986, 5(F).

OCR. "Friends of Eddie," *Lewiston [Maine] Daily Sun*," 11 March 1972, 4.

Owenby, Steve. "Adam-and-Eve-12," *National Review*, 26 November 1976, 1302-03.

Parker, Robert B., "Introduction," George V. Higgins, *The Easiest Thing in the World*, vii-viii.

Patrick, Vincent. "Smokeless Rooms," *New York Times Book Review*, 19 October 1997, 24.

Putney, Michael. "George Higgins: A First Novelist to Reckon With," *National Observer*, 1 April 1972, 21.

Ruppersburg, Hugh M. "George V. Higgins," *Dictionary of Literary Biography*, 2 (1978). 236-9.

Sandoff, Ivan. "Better than 'Godfather,'" *Worcester Sunday Telegraph*, 12 March 1972, 8(E).

Scrubbs, Wormwood [i.e., Richard Somervill]. "Witty Hiassen rates up there with 'John D.'" 7 February 1988, 4(C).

Seid, Marvin. "The Impostors," *Los Angeles Times Book Review*, 1 June 1986, 1, 10.

Sokolov, Raymond. "Two Class Acts," *Wall Street Journal*, 26 December 1989, 7(A).

Tucker, Clay. "George Higgins tale skillful but cynical," *Sunday Tennessean*, 11 October 1987, 7(F).

Veale, Scott, "Books in Brief: Fiction," *New York Times Book Review*, 19 May 1996, 24.

Vesterman, William. "Higgins's Trade, "*Language and Style*, 20 (1987), 223-29.

Von Hoffmann, Nicholas. "Making the Newsiest News," *TLS*, 21 February 1986, 183.

Woo, Adam. "Books Briefly," *Seattle Times*, 28 January 1990, 7(L).

— "And he scores!" *Seattle Times*, 24 January 1999, 8(M).

Worth, Robert. "Brilliant Ventriloquist," *Commonweal*, 25 March 1994, 24-5.

Yardley, Jonathan. "What Happens?" *New Republic*, 12 April 1975, 29.

Index

Joyce, James, 47, 54, 125; *Dubliners*, 39, 58, 124; "An Encounter," 58; *A Portrait of the Artist as a Young Man*, 54. 67, 107; "The Sisters," 39, 63; *Ulysses*, 6, 67
Just. Ward, 2
Kafka, Franz, 20, 106; "A Hunger Artist," 122
Kaplan, Frank L., 98
Keats, John, 23, 59—60, 71; "Autumn," 59; "Isabella, or the Pot of Basil," 59
Kennedy, William F., 9
Kipling, Rudyard, 118
Lardner, Ring, 72
Lawrence, D.H., 51, 90; "The Fox," 78; *Lady Chatterley's Lover*, 78; "Love on the Farm," 78; *Sons and Lovers*, 78; *Women in Love*, 78
Leavis, F.R., 57
le Carré, John, *The Constant Gardener*, 98
Leonard, Elmore, 4, 60, 93, 116
Lenin, V.I., 43,
Levenston, E.A., "Literary Dialect in George V. Higgins's 'Judgment of Deke Hunter,'" 83
Lewis, Peter, 34, 88, 90, 93
Liddy, G. Gordon, 1, 7
Locke, John, 30
Locke Ober Café (Boston), 1, 52, 95
Machiavelli, Niccolo, 124
Macdonald, Ross, 4, 48, 57, 59, 60, 78
Mailer, Norman, 19
Mamet, David, *American Buffalo*, 58
Mann, Thomas, 54, 67; *Doctor Faustus*, 119
Manning, Robert, 98
Mano, D. Keith, 72, 87
Marquand, John P., *The Late George Apley*, 4, 52
Marvell, Andrew, 96, 119
McBain, Ed, 65
McNeil, Robert, 87
McPherson, William, 107
Mencken, H.L., 26
Millar, Kenneth, see Macdonald, Ross
Miller, Arthur, *The Crucible*, 27, 58; *The Death of a Salesman*, 25, 45
Milton, John 54

Moore, Brian, *The Lonely Passion of Judith Hearne*, 67
Moore, Marianne, 127
Musil, Robert, 67
Mystic River (the movie), 4
Newman, Cardinal John Henry, 107
Nietzsche, Friedrich, 64
Occam, William of, 21
O'Connor, Edwin, *I Was Dancing*, 2; *The Last Hurrah*, 2, 123
O'Connor, Flannery, 19
OCR, 48
O'Hara, John, 22, 53—54, 57—58
O'Neill, Eugene, *The Iceman Cometh*, 51
O'Neill, Thomas P. "Tip," Jr., 4
Orr, Bobby, 24, 114
Orwell, George, 20
Owenby, Steve, 86—87
Parker, Robert B., 72, 93, 106
Pascal, Blaise, 21
Peterson, Henry, 26
Pinter, Harold, 84, 85, 90
Pirandello, Luigi, 28
Plato, 124
Poe, Edgar Allan, "The Mystery of Marie Rogët," 42, 57; "The Purloined Letter," 57
Porter, Cole, 96; *Kiss Me Kate*, 82
Putney, Michael, 48, 51
Queen, Ellery, 19
Rahv, Philip, *Image and Idea*, 119
Robinson, Edwin Arlington, 51; "Luke Havergall," 74
Rockwell, Norman, 76
Ross, James, *They Don't Dance Much*, 82
Roth, Philip, 19, 51, 81
Ruppersburg, Hugh M., 1, 85
Rushdie, Salman, 81
St. Augustine, 27, 60, 107
Sandoff, Ivan, 89
Sartre, Jean-Paul, 39
Sayers, Dorothy L., 19, 57
Scrubbs, Wormwood, see Somerville, Richard
Shaffer, Peter, *Equus*, 20
Shakespeare, William: *Hamlet*, 23, 96; *King Lear*, 96; *Measure for*

About the Author

Peter Wolfe is the Curators' Professor of English at the University of Missouri–St. Louis. A former Fulbright lecturer in Poland and India, he has also taught in Canada, New Zealand, Taiwan, Russia, and Australia. His many book subjects include Iris Murdoch, Rebecca West, August Wilson, Penelope Fitzgerald, and the *Twilight Zone* television series. Wolfe's 1993 book, *Alarms and Epitaphs: The Art of Eric Ambler*, won the first Armchair Detective Award for the best scholarly book in the mystery genre. His shorter work has appeared in the *New York Times Book Review*, the *Chicago Tribune, New Republic*, the *Calcutta Statesman, Modern Fiction Studies*, the *Los Angeles Times*, the *New Zealand Listener*, the *Weekend Australian*, and the *Sydney Morning Herald. Havoc in the Hub* is his twentieth book.